I WAS SIX THOUSAND MILES FROM HOME, in a combat zone, in one of the harshest places in the world. Unlike me, Fred *was* home. This compound was all he knew. And even though he'd probably never had a drink of clean water before or a scratch behind the ear, he was gentle and sweet. Looking down at him, I let go of worrying about the no-dog policy or when the next round of fighting would begin. For that moment, I felt like I was home, too.

YOUNG
READERS'
EDITION

CRAIG & FRED

A MARINE, A STRAY DOG, AND HOW THEY RESCUED EACH OTHER

CRAIG GROSSI

HARPER
An Imprint of HarperCollinsPublishers

Author's Note: Some names and identifying details of people in this book
have been changed in order to protect their privacy.

For a brief time in my life I walked among giants. This book is dedicated to those I walked alongside—to those who made it back and to those who did not. My story is not a profession of glory or grandeur; it is about how one person came to realize that it is not what happens to us but how we react that matters.

CHAPTER 1
LOOKS LIKE A FRED

IT WAS ALMOST MIDNIGHT when our helicopter arrived in Sangin, Afghanistan. In the final moments before we touched down, no one spoke. We secured our packs and turned on our night-vision goggles. We were about to be dropped several miles from a compound that would become our base. There was no time to waste: We had to hike to the site, then spend the rest of the night filling sandbags and preparing for the attack that would almost certainly come at sunrise.

I was an intelligence collector for the United States Marine Corps, so my job was to learn as much as I could from the villagers about the Taliban, the fundamentalist political group that was waging war in Afghanistan. If we captured a Taliban fighter, I was the only one in the unit who could question him.

The guys I was heading out with were Recon marines, reconnaissance forces. My expertise was in communication; theirs was in combat. They were the real deal—an elite force of special operations guys who were tough and experienced. They were like professional athletes, and smart, too. To earn their trust, I needed to prove that I was able to keep up on long nighttime patrols and in gunfights. I also needed to show that I brought something to the battlefield that they couldn't provide themselves.

I had been on another mission in an agricultural town in southern Afghanistan, but I knew this was going to be a different fight. In the previous mission, I had served with a British Royal Marine named Jack. He was supposed to come with us to Sangin, but he changed his plans.

"I'm not going back there," he'd said. He had served there a few years earlier when British forces first secured the area. "It's the kind of place where you turn a corner and there's two Taliban guys standing there. One's got an RPG"—that's a rocket-propelled grenade—"and the other's got a machine gun, and they're just waiting to light you up. The place is bonkers."

Sangin had that reputation. The Taliban were bolder there because it was an important location for poppy farming, and the opium trade helped fund the Taliban. We expected them to have a lot of fighters and a lot of firepower.

The Taliban controlled the families in the villages, who had no other choice but to go along with what they were told. The Taliban took what they wanted, shutting down the local economy. These villages were extremely poor. Often, the Taliban were the only ones who owned anything of much material value, from sneakers to cell phones to the little Honda motorcycles they drove around. When they needed food, they'd show up at markets and bakeries and take what they pleased. If a motorcycle broke down, they'd find the only mechanic in town and take the parts or make him fix the bike at gunpoint. They ruined weddings, breaking musical instruments and punishing guests for dancing. They recruited—or just took—young boys to join their forces.

With a thud, the helicopter landed in a cloud of dust. We stepped out into the night, rifles up. The desert earth was firm under my boots, and a thin layer of silky dust washed over everything like water. I tried not to cough. The helicopter rotors whipped up a heavy haze of dirt before lifting the vehicle back into the sky.

There's nothing like the sound of that hum disappearing into the distance. At that point it's just you and the guys on the ground, with no machine to protect you or whisk you away. That's when it gets real.

We started moving, single file to avoid IEDs—improvised explosive devices—and bombs. All I heard was the sound of our boots scuffing against the dirt and our packs shifting on our backs. With very little light pollution, Afghanistan is supposed to be ideal for stargazing, but the dust in Sangin never settled. Overhead the dark sky looked like a smudged impressionist painting.

We walked two or three miles, over rolling hills, heading west. In all, there were about sixty guys—three platoons of marines, plus "attachments" like me and the Explosive Ordnance Disposal team (EOD) trained to find and dispose of bombs, as well as members of the Afghan National Army. Our gear and backpacks were heavy—seventy pounds or more—but we were well trained. After a while, my heart rate steadied as my body got used to the idea of being in Sangin.

When we came up to the compound, we saw an elderly man waiting in the doorway. We only established bases in compounds that were occupied. If folks were already living there and hadn't been blown up, that was a good sign that the place wasn't rigged with bombs.

Ali, the interpreter on the mission, and I walked up to talk to the man. Ali had been on the previous mission with me, and we'd gotten close. He was from Afghanistan but had moved to the United States years ago. Now, he'd returned to help his homeland, and to make a decent living for his wife and newborn baby back in Arizona.

We approached the villager and shook his hand. I explained who we were and that we were here to help—and that we would need his family to move to another compound. Often, families like his were nomads, moving from place to place to work as share-croppers. In this case, the elderly man told us he and his family hadn't been there very long, and he kindly agreed to relocate.

He opened the small metal door, and we filed in. Some of us got to work preparing the compound, while others helped the man and his family move a few hundred yards away to a neighboring site, bringing their cows and goats with them.

The compound was large. Its thick mud walls were about twelve feet high. Inside, there were a few basic structures, like little huts—small buildings made of packed mud. We spent the night filling green plastic sandbags, assembly-line style. Using a collapsible shovel, I scooped dust and dirt into the bags, then another guy would carry them over to the marines on the roof, who would hoist them onto the tops of the clay buildings. The sandbags—which were bulletproof when filled—were used to build a shield to protect the guys while they fired on the enemy. Down below, we dug small windows into the main wall so that we could see out and shoot to defend ourselves.

We worked all night. When the sun came up, I could see the wide, sweeping desert that stretched out to the east. To the west, the compound overlooked Highway 611 and, beyond it, the Green Zone. We called it the Green Zone because that's where the Helmand River flowed, giving way to lush, green farmland. Fields of corn and poppies spread out on either side of the river, along with an extensive network of irrigation canals.

"Highway" 611 was actually a dirt road that ran north to south. It was a regular site of bomb attacks. The highway divided the irrigated land in the Green Zone from the scorched desert where we had established our post.

The Taliban controlled the Green Zone. Our mission was to drive them out so that coalition forces—engineers and soldiers from the United States and other countries working to bring peace to Afghanistan—could safely make their way up Highway 611. After the area was secured, the road could be cleared of bombs, allowing a much-needed generator to be delivered to a dam in the north. Once functional, it would provide electricity to the entire region.

Sangin is so remote and rural that many Afghan people refuse to go there. It's tribal land, home to fewer than 15,000 residents, most of them farmers who live largely without access to formal education or electricity. That's part of what makes the region so susceptible to Taliban abuse and control.

A few weeks before we arrived, the Third Battalion, Fifth Marines—also called 3/5 or Darkhorse—had faced heavy fighting in Sangin. In the first week, they lost ten marines. We were here not only to help clear out the Taliban from around the highway, but also to take some pressure off the 3/5 marines in the south.

My main objective in Sangin was to understand the situation on the ground from a villager's point of view. I needed to get to know the locals. What did people call themselves here? Which tribes did they belong to? How did they earn a living? And how were the Taliban affecting their lives? By building relationships, I'd be able to get critical information from people. I also wanted to create a database of people's names, tribes, family members, jobs, and locations.

In the daylight, two marines took up post on the rooftop position, turning their binoculars toward the fields. The Taliban almost certainly knew we were here. If they hadn't figured out our exact location yet, they would soon.

From the roof, one of the marines shouted, "I've got movement! Northwest!"

I looked through one of the openings in the wall. I saw people emerging from the edge of the fields and crossing into the desert, coming toward us. They were moving slowly and carrying things—sacks of rice and bags of belongings. I saw someone pushing a wheel-barrow carrying an old woman and another leading a donkey with blankets and buckets hanging on either side. These weren't Taliban fighters. They were villagers. They were leaving the Green Zone, their possessions on their backs.

They kept coming. For two hours, we watched as dozens of people made their way out of the Green Zone to the dusty cluster of compounds near ours. They realized that if they stayed where they were, they risked being turned into targets by the Taliban. Fighters often occupied private homes for shelter while they launched attacks on us. It was a well-known Taliban tactic to increase civilian deaths.

The morning sky swelled with light. Already the dust had worked its way into my hair, skin, and clothes. Everything had the same stale smell. I grabbed a bottle of water and splashed my face, then started my favorite ritual: preparing instant coffee. My sister had given me a little stove that could heat water in sixty seconds. It was magic.

Across the compound, I saw Top, our leader and master sergeant, doing the same thing. A twenty-year veteran with a square jaw and bricks for fists, Top rarely uttered more than two words at once.

As I lifted the hot cup of coffee to my lips, I heard it: the distinct, overpowering thunder of an attack.

Directly overhead, the sky screamed, *WHOOSH!*

I looked up as a rocket soared through the air, followed by another. They seemed to sail by slowly, as if they were floating. Their paths crisscrossed, and I realized they must have been launched from different locations. One buzzed off into the distance, missing our compound.

Another cracked open into a sharp, deafening explosion at the far end of the compound. It rattled my teeth and rang in my ears.

I looked over at Top, who was moving into action. He ran into our makeshift control center, one of the little clay rooms in the center of the compound, to get on the radio. Around me, guys were putting on their gear. I grabbed my stuff and rushed to the wall to peer out the hole. I saw desert and dust. Nothing.

Behind me, the west wall—the one facing the Green Zone—was getting all the action. Rifle rounds hit the clay, sending dirt flying. The guys on the roof shouted to one another, preparing to return fire.

I heard reports over the radio: We were nearly surrounded. Taliban fire was coming from 270 degrees around us. At first, the guys on the roof were taking some machine gun and small arms fire. But then I heard their voices change as they reported that "some fire" was now "*accurate* fire."

We had about eight guys returning fire on what was easily a few hundred Taliban. The rounds peppered the sandbags with a near continuous *rat-a-tat-tat-tat-tat-tat-tat*.

The guys had to duck down. You never want to get pinned down like that. It means you can't beat back the enemy, and it's going to get worse.

Above, the sky was cloudless and blue.

"*Corpsman!*" Someone was calling for the medical specialist.

I heard an urgent call come over the radio from the rooftop position nearest the Green Zone. I looked up and saw Joe lying limp beside his partner, Aaron.

Aaron unbuckled Joe's helmet while rounds continued to whizz overhead. He checked for injuries but didn't see any blood. Joe looked okay. Aaron checked the helmet again and saw two holes where the bullet had gone in and out.

Dizzy and confused, Joe backed down the ladder. I helped him down, and another marine examined his head, parting his short hair with his fingers. The round had skimmed through the top of his helmet without hitting Joe's head at all.

This first attack didn't last long—less than a half hour—but it felt like forever. One minute it was chaos; the next minute, quiet. I was soaked in sweat, wearing heavy armor and a helmet in 100-degree heat, and my mouth was an oven. But I was alive.

Within an hour, the next attack came. It was similar to the first. The Taliban liked to start with something dynamic—using a big, powerful weapon—hoping to maximize casualties. They always launched attacks from at least two locations, followed by mortars and gunfire. Then they'd recover and reposition, launching the next attack about an hour later. It would continue like this until sundown.

It was the same, day after day. Guys took shifts on the roofs. We took fire. We returned it. For a short span of time in the afternoons, when the sun rose high in the sky and it got to be 115 degrees, the desert fell quiet. It was unbearable to do anything, and for a couple hours, the Taliban stopped their assault.

During this period, we cleaned our guns and

ate our MREs—meals ready to eat—which were vacuum-sealed, military-issued space food, such as spaghetti, meatballs, chili mac, chicken and rice, and meat loaf. Sometimes we played cards and took naps. We tried to make jokes, cool down, clean off. We were filthy, covered in dirt freckles, little specks of dust on our skin that no baby wipe could get off. Our "bathroom" was a chicken coop where we did our business in little silver bags with deodorizing powder, then tossed the bags into a burn pit. In less time than you might think, this became our new normal.

It was between Taliban attacks that I spotted him. I was hot and exhausted, trying to stay cool in sandals and thin green running shorts. I was refilling my water bottle when I saw a goofy-looking dog trot across the compound. With his short legs and puppy-like pep, he looked nothing like other stray dogs I'd seen in Afghanistan. Most were tall and bulky, and they moved around in packs, aggressive over territory and scavenged scraps.

This dog was different. He didn't have a pack. He was alone. He pranced nonchalantly in the dust, tail bobbing and snout held high, as if he was particularly proud of the scrap of food he was carrying. There was something innocent about him, like he was unaffected by life in a combat zone.

When we first arrived at the compound, I questioned the old man about a couple dogs that were hanging around. "Are they yours?" I asked. If so, we'd help transport them to the family's new compound, along with the livestock.

"No, no, no," he told us. It would have been unusual for a farmer in Sangin to have a pet dog. The villagers loved animals and took great care of their livestock, but they were focused on surviving and on feeding their families. They couldn't afford to feed and care for a pet.

After the family left and we moved in, the goofy dog stayed. It was almost as if this was his compound. I stood and watched him flop down in his spot under the bushes. Beside him I could see other scraps he'd accumulated: food wrappers, sticks, bones.

I put down my water bottle, picked up a piece of beef jerky, and started walking over to him. When the dog realized I was coming his way, he stopped eating and looked at me. He watched as I approached, squinting to shield his eyes from the dust and sun.

A few steps away from him, I paused.

"Hey, buddy," I said. "How's it going?"

He seemed to be studying me. There was something expressive, almost human-like, about his big, light brown eyes. For a moment, we looked at each other. I heard a quiet *thwap thwap thwap*. A little cloud of dust kicked up into the air behind him. I couldn't believe it: he was wagging his tail.

I took it as an invitation to move closer. I crouched down to get a better look at him. The dog's fur was mostly white with large spots of light orange-brown markings. He had floppy ears and a long snout with a big black nose. As he looked at me, his eyebrows twitched from side to side, curious. He continued to wag his tail, and his expression was soft and easy, like he was smiling.

The dog seemed happy, but he was covered with black bugs the size of dimes. They were buzzing around him and burrowing into the fur on his face and neck.

I extended my arm, holding out the piece of beef jerky. "Here you go, buddy," I said.

The dog stood up and shook, as if to rid himself of as many bugs as possible before getting near me. He took a few steps forward, his nose leading the way, and inspected my offering before carefully pulling it from my hand with his front teeth. I laughed watching him chew the jerky. Most dogs I knew didn't bother chewing treats before sending them down the hatch.

"Well, you've got better manners than most, don't you?" I said, and extended my other hand so he could give it a few sniffs. With his permission, I massaged my fingers into the fur around his neck and under his ears.

It was coarse and matted. It felt unnaturally stiff, almost like a dirty pair of jeans. But the dog happily leaned into me, pleased with the neck rub. I wondered if it was the first time he'd ever been touched.

I'd always wanted a dog as a kid. I even went so far as to buy a leash with my own money. I knocked on the neighbors' doors after school, volunteering to walk their dogs for free. Some of them actually let me. My favorite pup was an old basset hound named Irene. She had oversized paws and huge floppy ears. When I walked her, she'd trot ahead of me, out at the end of the leash, with her snout high in the air, taking in all the smells she could. This dusty pup with his long body and short legs made me think of her.

Before I got carried away with him, though, I stopped myself. Cozying up to dogs was off-limits in Afghanistan. When I first arrived in country, I sat through two days of orientation. We learned the rules. No alcohol. No saluting superiors (to avoid signaling who was in charge, which put them at greater risk). No dogs. Some wild dogs had rabies. Get caught with a stray dog, and the dog will be euthanized—put to death—no questions asked.

I knew the rules. I was also still trying to prove myself to the Recon guys. I had to prove my worth on this mission, not sit around in the dust with a dog.

With that in mind, I reluctantly got up. The dog just stood there, looking up. "Okay, buddy," I said. I turned and headed back toward my corner of the compound.

But after taking just a few steps, I felt a little nudge at the back of my ankle. I looked down to see the dog looking up at me with a toothy grin, tail wagging again. From across the compound, another marine had been watching our exchange. "Looks like you made a friend!" he shouted.

I thought he said, "Looks like a *Fred*!"

The name stuck.

Fred trotted along behind me back to the makeshift campsite where I had my sleeping mat. I didn't try to stop him. There wasn't much harm in giving him another piece of jerky and some water.

I grabbed a large tin bowl that was lying around— it had probably been for the cows—and filled it with water from my canteen. Placing it down in front of Fred, I watched as he licked the thing dry. I stood over him and smiled. Just like he'd taken the jerky from me with a gentle tug, he drank water the same way, with polite little laps.

Jim, the medical specialist, had been watching Fred, too. He got up from his spot in the shade and came over, taking a closer look at the bugs on Fred's neck. He pulled tweezers from his fanny pack and, pointing to the bugs, said, "Why don't you hold him steady, and we'll see if I can get some of these bloodsuckers off?"

The two of us crouched in the dirt. I sat cross-legged and pulled Fred toward me, holding him by the shoulders. The bugs, like flying ticks, were digging into Fred's fur and attaching to his hide. Getting them out meant Jim was going to have to pull them from his skin.

"Careful, dude," I said, as Jim narrowed in on one, closing down on it with the tweezers. I didn't know how Fred was going to react. In one quick motion, Jim yanked hard and, between the prongs of the tweezers, pulled away the first bug along with a clump of Fred's fur. I braced myself for a yowl or nip from Fred, but he just sat there, unbothered. Jim and I exchanged looks. Carefully, he kept going, pulling out one bug at a time.

Patiently, Fred just sat there, letting us do our work.

When we finished, a tiny bug graveyard had piled up in the dirt beside us. Jim gave Fred a pat on the top of the head and stood up. "Wow," he said. "I can't believe he let us do that."

Fred shook again, then walked to my sleeping mat. He stepped over the edge of the bug net and climbed in, pawing at the material to arrange it how he wanted. It was as if he'd done it a hundred times before. Content with the arrangement, he settled in, let out a sigh, and blinked his eyes closed. I was caked in dirt, too, so I didn't mind if he wanted a spot on my bed. Jim and I laughed.

"Little guy is making himself right at home!" he said.

I leaned over and zipped up the bug net for my new friend. I was six thousand miles from home, in a combat zone, in one of the harshest places in the world. Unlike me, Fred *was* home. This compound was all he knew. And even though he'd probably never had a drink of clean water before or a scratch behind the ear, he was gentle and sweet. Looking down at him, I let go of worrying about the no-dog policy or when the next round of fighting would begin. For that moment, I felt like I was home, too.

CHAPTER 2
SERGEANT FRED

FRED BECAME POPULAR in the compound. Within forty-eight hours, the guys started calling him Freddy or Freddy Zone, a combination of his name and *combat zone*. "Hey, Freddy Zone!" we'd call out when the compound was hot and quiet. Fred would wander over for a pat and a treat, happy for the attention.

I began to share my food with him. One day I smeared peanut butter on the roof of his mouth, and he smacked his lips, trying to reach every last bit with his tongue while I giggled. He was like a little brother. It turned out the other marines weren't worried about my interest in Fred; they wanted to hang out with him, too.

One of the guys found a piece of rope and used it to play tug-of-war with Fred, getting him all riled up. Fred started to get vocal, barking and howling with excitement. Sometimes he'd bare his teeth, too, which cracked us up. He'd flash his big white grin, growling to try to seem fierce, but with his funny short legs and sweet personality, we didn't buy it.

Our favorite topic of conversation was Fred's goofy looks. Not only was he much smaller than any other dogs we came across in Afghanistan—he weighed less than thirty pounds—but his short legs were an oddity we loved. Being low to the ground didn't hurt Fred's pride. He trotted around the compound like a show dog, head up, tail bouncing, paws flicking the dirt. He had an irresistible combination of innocence and confidence.

After Joe was shot on the first day, he spent nearly a week holed up in a little room in the compound that functioned as an aid station. Joe was okay, but he had quite a concussion. He needed to be taken out of Sangin, but in the meantime, the doc kept him in the cool, dark room so he could rest. Nauseated and suffering from the worst headache of his life, Joe lay on a mat in pain, in and out of sleep, waiting. The Taliban had ambushed another group of marines, so Joe had to wait days for a helicopter out.

On the first day, Fred showed up in the doorway to the aid station. He paused and looked at Joe, then walked up to him. Leaning in with his hot breath, Fred sniffed Joe's face, pressing his wet nose into his cheek. Then, he lay down next to him, resting his head right across Joe's chest. Fred let out a sigh and looked up, meeting Joe's eyes, as if asking, "You okay?" Slowly Fred closed his eyes and just lay there with Joe. After a few minutes, Fred got up and left.

Every few hours, Fred came back and went through the same routine, checking on Joe. Fred kept an eye on him for days. It was clear there was something remarkable about this dog.

During firefights, none of us could afford to get distracted by Fred's whereabouts. We assumed he could take care of himself. Once, though, the Taliban were unusually effective during an attack, landing a mortar round just outside the wall of our compound. When it went off, it felt like the earth was about to split open. Our mortar team and spotters remained posted while the rest of us took cover in the command center. We huddled together, waiting. Then, through the open doorway, I spotted Fred. He was grazing through the burn pit looking for scraps like he always did. His nose was to the ground as he nudged through dirt like a lazy detective looking for clues.

The guys and I looked at one another, all with the same mental image: a well-placed round landing on our new friend, sending him into the air in bits and pieces.

"Fred!" we shouted. "*Fred!*"

The dog continued to pick through the garbage.

"Get back here!"

Finally, Fred looked up at us. He blinked in the sun, looking mildly confused, then promptly put his nose back to the earth and kept hunting for scraps.

Overhead, one of our spotters on the rooftop post yelled, "Incoming!" and we braced for impact. This time, the round landed at the far end of the compound, sending a bone-rattling shock wave through the place. That got Fred's attention. He took off, kicking up a cloud of dust as he went, darting right into our shelter and wiggling his way to safety between our legs.

In those early days, while Fred was becoming part of the team, I worried that befriending the dog might be putting him at risk. If the command perceived him to be a distraction or threat in any way, he'd have to go.

In the compound, I kept my eye on Top, the command master sergeant, who watched us play with Fred. Top was a huge, quiet marine; we'd probably exchanged about four words. One night on the previous mission,

I'd helped him carry his backpack across a canal during a patrol. I was standing in hip-deep water, so the guys could pass me their packs, then leap across. Top walked up and looked at me. Holding out his pack, he said, "It might be heavy," then dropped it into my arms. The weight of the thing sank me four inches into the mud. It must have been ninety pounds, almost twice as heavy as the others, full of radio gear and two weeks' worth of backup batteries the size of bricks. I thought it was going to crush me like a paperweight when a team-mate on the other side took it from me. Then Top leapt across the canal, picked it up, and flung it across his back like it was a lunch box. He was that strong.

And he was tough. I swear we never saw him eat or sleep. Top had been in the corps since the nineties, deploying twice to Iraq and to Somalia. He was a real leader, and we all respected him. I knew he'd do what he needed to do to keep us safe. That included making sure a stray dog didn't compromise our mission.

I had all this on my mind one afternoon as I sat in the shade, eating the last bites of my lunch. Fred was shuffling around, sniffing our stuff, and peeing on things. Then I saw him wander off to look for a shady spot of his own. Across the compound, Top leaned in the doorway of the command center, finishing off his lunch. Fred started to walk toward Top, panting slightly in the heat. The bugs had left him alone since we'd plucked them away, but his fur was still caked in dirt. Clouds of dust poofed off his back as he walked.

Fred reached Top and looked up. They stared at each other for a minute, then Fred dropped his hind legs and sat down next to the big marine. The two of them gazed across the compound in the same direction, almost like they were chewing on the same thought. I wondered how this was going to play out. This was the first time I had seen Fred and Top interact with each other.

Top scooped one last bite of whatever he was eating into his mouth, then squatted next to Fred. He put the plastic food container in front of Fred's mouth, as if to say, "Here." Fred wiggled his nose and licked up the last bit of Top's meal. Top wore sunglasses, so it was hard to make out his expression, but I thought I saw a hint of a smile.

Atta boy, I thought. Fred was making friends in high places.

In Sangin, the Recon marines were discretionary shooters. That meant they had the authority and responsibility to decide when to shoot first. Most of them were higher ranking and had been in the military for years. This sent a message to the Taliban that we were serious.

As a result, after those first few days, the fighting became less frequent. There was talk of starting night patrols into the Green Zone. We could scout out the area, talk to the villagers, and try to get a better idea of what was going on. It was time for me to do my job.

Twelve of us would go out on a carefully pre-mapped route. The first cluster of compounds we planned to approach was only about a mile away, but we would follow a three-mile route to get there. We had to avoid established roads, paths, and bridges, which were rigged with a network of bombs. Instead, we cut through fields and waded through canals, moving in a single file and creating our own path. We wouldn't return on the same route we took out. Meanwhile, Top would stay near the radio to receive status updates as we went. We'd leave in the dark and return before the sun came up, staying out no more than eight hours.

As the sun set, the twelve of us lined up our kits along the wall—body armor, helmets, ammunition, and night-vision goggles. I also carried a notepad and a small battery-powered camera. We'd only been in the compound a few days, but it felt like a safe haven. The thought of leaving it to walk straight toward the Taliban made my stomach churn.

Before leaving I sat on an ammo crate and ate dinner: spaghetti. It was my favorite MRE; the other choices were beef stroganoff, chili mac, and chicken and rice.

My paternal grandparents were Italian, and I smiled thinking about what Nonie and Pop-Pop would have thought of the limp noodles and plain sauce. Beside me, Ali, the Afghan translator, drank chai and used my satellite telephone to make a quick call to his family. I wasn't supposed to let anyone use my phone, but it was worth it to bend the rules for Ali, who had a family back home.

As Ali wrapped up his call, he pointed toward my gear and smiled. "Fred's keeping track of you," he said.

I looked up. Fred had made a bed out of my stuff, curling up right on my flak vest.

"He's your boss," Ali laughed.

I smiled. "He wants to know when I leave so he can jump into my sleeping bag," I said. I wondered if the dog was getting too attached to me. Fred was winning over all the marines one by one, but I felt like we had a special connection.

The sun disappeared on the horizon in an orange blaze, and after a few hours, when the sky was black, we started suiting up. Fred had gone off somewhere, and I tried to stay focused. Top stood by the tiny metal door that opened in the direction of the Green Zone. One by one, we ducked through and stepped out, Top counting us as we went.

The night was cool and quiet. Through my

night-vision equipment, the desert looked like the surface of the moon cast in shades of green. Each time my boot hit the ground, a little poof of dust erupted around it. The looseness of the dirt made it easy for the Taliban to plant bombs under the surface. I looked toward the guy in front of me, then glanced down to watch where I was stepping, then scanned the horizon and checked my flanks through the night-vision goggles. I thought about how I'd introduce myself to villagers and the questions I'd ask.

At the edge of the desert, we came to a ridge that overlooked the lush fields below. I could feel the change in climate. The air was moist, and I thought I could make out the sound of the river. As we walked along the ridge, I suddenly caught a glimpse of something moving toward my left. Without thinking, I turned, aiming my rifle.

It was Fred. He scampered along the way he always did, with light feet, head held high, and his tail bobbing up and down. He had the air of a tour guide showing a group of visitors around his turf, even though none of us had ever seen him leave the compound. The other guys had noticed him too, and we all just smiled in disbelief.

This dog is full of surprises, I thought.

At the planned location, two marines made their

way down the ridge. There was a canal at the bottom that looked fairly wide, and they'd figure out how best to cross it. The rest of us formed a protective circle, took a knee, and scanned the horizon. Fred, who until then had kept his distance, came up and nudged me on the hip. I gave him a quick scratch behind the ear, feeling the familiar dingy fur on his warm neck, and then watched as he went up to the next guy. He moved along quietly, offering nudges and receiving gentle pats. Our little field dog was herding his marines.

The guys at the bottom of the ridge radioed for us to follow. We were officially crossing into the Green Zone.

We filed down the steep cliff and prepared to cross the canal. One at a time, we slid down a muddy bank and waded through. The water was cold and deep; it came up to my waist. I held my rifle overhead and put my notebook in my mouth. The mud on the bed of the canal suctioned the soles of my boots with each step, so I tried to move quickly to keep from sinking. At the opposite side, the guys pulled me out, then I waited to help the next guy. As I turned around, I looked back to see that Fred was in the canal, swimming across to us. His snout and tail were high above the water, and I could see the effort of his little legs paddling along. He didn't want to miss out on anything.

The terrain in the Green Zone was different from the desert. The ground was muddy and damp, and on the horizon, corn and poppy fields shimmered in the moonlight. The only sound came from our boots slapping the mud.

We made our way past a small village with a few abandoned compounds. A pack of dogs began howling and moaning when we walked by. They were big, much bigger than Fred, and their sharp barks rattled off the walls of the buildings behind them. A few came close to our patrol, their heads hung low and their fur raised along the ridge of their backs. They looked like wolves mixed with hyenas. We sped up so that they'd quiet down. I looked around for Fred, anxious that he'd start barking or fighting with the other dogs. I glanced behind me, and there he was, moving along quickly at my heel in silence, head down, eyes ahead. Back at the compound later that night, the guys talked, and we decided that it was that moment—on top of everything else—that truly blew us away. It was as if Fred knew how to be a marine. He had ignored any instinct he might have had to bark back at the pack of dogs. We were quiet, so he was, too.

We made our way through, carefully crossing three more canals, until finally we reached our destination village. I was soaked and muddy, and the night was cold, but my nerves and our trek kept my blood warm. It was time for us to get to work. Most of the villages we went to hadn't been mapped out, and we needed to know the names of the villages and what tribes the people were from.

The first compound we approached had a big metal green door. It was too risky to walk right up to it and knock. The marines covered our position, looking out, as I tossed clumps of dirt at the door. The metal vibrated in response, creating a high-pitched sound. Ali said that we wanted to talk; he spoke in Pashto, one of two official languages of Afghanistan.

The door opened, and an older man in a white robe leaned out. Ali spoke to him, quickly and quietly explaining who we were and asking if we could talk. Because he was so cooperative, Ali asked if he could gather a few of his neighbors so that we could have a *shura,* or a group meeting. The man stepped out from behind the door, and we walked to the next compound, then another. One of the neighbors rolled out a blanket in a nearby field, and we sat to talk. The Recon guys fanned out wide, almost out of sight, standing post. Fred walked around at a distance, sniffing the ground and looking out.

The conversation was brief. The men answered our questions about what tribe they were part of, their ages, and their names. They didn't have much to say about the Taliban. It was possible that they really didn't have any information, or that they didn't want to get involved. I took pictures of each person for my report, and we thanked them for gathering with us.

We went to another village before making our way back, taking a long, wandering route to the compound. The terrain in the Green Zone was complex and exhausting, but we were safe. As we ducked through the doorway, Top stood waiting as he had done when we left. He greeted us each by name. "Well done, Craig," he said to me. Fred, who had stayed with us for the entire journey, scampered through. Smiling, Top said, "Well done, Sergeant Fred."

We assembled in Top's command center to compare notes. I took a seat in the back on a bag of rice. The red glow of a lantern lit up our tired, mud-smudged faces, and the green glimmer of the radio flickered in the corner. Top looked around and counted heads. Someone joked, "Where's Fred?" As if on cue, he came trotting into the room, winding his way through our boots. He found his way to Top, lay down using Top's boot as a headrest, and let out a sigh as if to say, "I'm here."

Afterward, Fred showed up right as I sat down on my sleeping mat. I untied my boots and left them beside me, stacking my pants on top so I could jump in at a moment's notice. Next to them sat my body armor, my helmet, extra ammunition, a rifle, and my camera. I took off my watch, placing it next to my pillow, and as I swung my legs around to settle in, Fred jumped in, too. He took a couple turns, pawed at the sleeping bag, then settled behind my knees, resting his head on my thigh. When I was a kid, sometimes our family cat, Patches, would sleep in the same spot. Having Fred there felt familiar. It was a little piece of home.

In Afghanistan, that's what Fred offered all of us. Each time he curled up in one of our sleeping bags or trotted across the compound or let us scratch him behind the ears, we got an escape from the combat zone we were in. In those moments, it was just us and Fred.

The next day, I was on a rooftop post looking through my binoculars into the green fields in the distance. One of the guys said, "Hey, look."

I looked down to where he was pointing. A man and woman were about thirty feet away, walking toward our compound. The man led and the woman followed, leading their donkey, packed with bags of rice, rugs, and buckets on its back.

We were happy to see them. We hadn't seen villagers come so close to the compound, and, after days of firefights, it seemed like a good sign that people were out in the middle of the day. Maybe we'd driven away enough Taliban for them to regain some freedom of movement.

Then I heard a loud explosion. It felt like a clap of thunder. I flinched and ducked my head, then looked over to where the couple had been. The man stood in his long white shirt and pants, motionless. Behind him, where the woman and donkey had been, a black cloud of smoke rose from the ground. The bitter smell of ammonia hung in the air. The hair on my arms stood up. The woman had stepped on an IED.

I rushed down from the roof. Below, Ali was already talking with some of the Afghan commandos and a few marines. Ali thought we should speak with the man to make sure he knew that coalition forces hadn't killed his wife. We could also help him. In the Islamic religion, only another Muslim should handle a dead body. Because Ali and the Afghan commandos were Muslim, they could offer to help gather the woman's remains. One of the Afghan commandos went to get a bedsheet. I put on my kit, and we walked out.

After the explosion, the man stood frozen for several minutes, looking at the blast site. Now he was moving about, collecting his wife's body. The commandos approached him with the sheet and offered to help. Ali joined them, telling him how sorry we were. The man, understandably, seemed shocked. He spoke rapidly, and I couldn't follow what was being said. For a long time, the men spoke in Pashto, the local language. I had learned only some key phrases in Pashto before going to Afghanistan. I waited nearby, tense and hot.

When it felt like the right moment, I joined the conversation. I offered my sympathies and made it clear that his wife had been killed by the Taliban. He understood.

I sucked in my breath and, feeling sick, made a final request. It was my job to record and report casualties caused by the Taliban. I explained the situation and asked if I could photograph his wife's body. The man agreed. He opened the bedsheet, and I took several images. My chest was so tight it was hard to breathe. I wanted to throw up. It took everything I had to remain composed.

Back in the compound, we gathered to discuss what had happened. It was clear that there were bombs much closer to our compound than we had realized. We'd practically walked over that same area on our way out for night patrol. We were almost certainly surrounded by many more hidden explosives.

As we were talking, I spotted Fred. He came trotting across the compound with something in his mouth. If you've ever seen a dog with a new toy—totally gleeful and proud, practically squirming with joy—that's how Fred looked. He plopped down and started gnawing, happy as ever. Then I realized what it was: a charred piece of donkey leg, from the hoof to the knee, almost as big as he was.

"Ugh, Fred!" I ran over and pulled the thing from his mouth, throwing it over the wall. "No!" I shouted sternly, looking at his confused puppy face.

The next day, I found the leg at the end of my sleeping bag. I picked it up and threw it over the wall again, hoping that was the end of it. But Fred somehow found it, once again, and brought it back in. Over the next few days, he continued to leave it around the compound, sometimes on different guys' sleeping mats, and we continued throwing it over the wall. We couldn't be mad: Fred didn't know anything about the Taliban or tragedy or war. It was his innocence—especially in the dark moments—that kept us going.

CHAPTER 3
INTO THE GREEN ZONE

ALI AND I PATROLLED every night. I wanted to build relationships with as many villagers as possible. It was helpful for us to have positive face-to-face interactions with families so that when they had information about the Taliban, they'd be more likely to tell us. We didn't want the villagers to think of us as well-armed mysterious soldiers up on a hill. On patrol, we had the chance to introduce ourselves as real people, there to help.

Once, Ali and I climbed into a compound, using a ladder, and startled an older man as he walked across the courtyard. "It's okay, grandfather," Ali said in Pashto. "We're here to talk." A few other marines kept watch from the roof while the old man brought his family to the courtyard, where we all sat in a circle. There were nine or ten people gathered there.

I took the night-vision goggles from my helmet and handed them to one of the kids. She was amazed by how they worked. She lifted them to her face, pulled them away, then looked through again, smiling in disbelief. A teenage boy passed around chai tea. From my pack, I took out photos of my family, showing pictures of my parents and sister. One picture showed my sister, Sarah, holding her dog, Herbie, a little Yorkie mix with short, shiny brown hair, a smooshed snout, and a peppy personality. For whatever reason, the Afghan villagers found the picture of Herbie hilarious. This group was no exception. The kids giggled at the little dog, cracking up until they lost their breath.

I told them we were here because we knew the Taliban were making life difficult, and we wanted to help get things back to normal so that they could open their schools and shops again. We knew that in small villages like this, the Taliban spread rumors about us. They told the villagers that the September 11 attacks were retaliation for the United States coming to their country, not the other way around.

When we had a chance to talk with people, I was always amazed by their kindness and understanding.

They listened and asked questions, and they were grateful for our presence. It gave me hope that our mission was meaningful and would have a positive impact on the Afghan people. The conversations helped me, too. I enjoyed them. Even with the language barrier, I found I could connect with people. Sometimes when I was talking with the villagers, I no longer felt like I was in a battle zone. Even though their homes looked different from mine, I felt welcomed.

As the patrols went on, the days started to run together. I wrote reports each morning after returning from the overnight patrols. I would try to nap, but between the heat and Taliban attacks, my sleep was often interrupted. Before I knew it, it was time to go on patrol again.

After his first expedition out, Fred continued to follow me on night patrols. He'd silently trot next to our patrol line, about thirty feet to the left or right, stopping when we stopped, crossing canals when we crossed canals, and struggling up muddy banks right alongside us. He was so quiet and agile that no one questioned his company. He didn't distract us or interfere with our work. Instead, he was a comfort, our little patrol dog looking out for us.

One night that changed. On our way to a village in

the Green Zone, we cut through a cornfield. The cornstalks were twice our height and as close together as the hair on our heads. It was perfect concealment for moving around undetected. It was also perfect for getting lost. As we walked through the fields, each member of the patrol had to keep an eye on the guy in front of him to avoid becoming disoriented. Because the corn was so dense and difficult to navigate, Fred didn't follow us in. Instead, he found a path around the field so that he could meet us on the other side. It made me nervous. One wrong step, and Fred could trigger a bomb.

As we emerged from the corn, we were surrounded by hundreds of acres of barren fields. The open space was less than ideal. There was nothing to conceal us, and the moon made the night brighter than usual. Out in the open, we were sitting ducks. A single Taliban fighter would have no problem taking out multiple members of our patrol. We got on the move, quickly.

Fred showed up and trotted along on his own path out ahead of us. As I watched him, a strange, unfamiliar noise shattered the quiet of the night. It took a second for me to recognize the sound: Fred barking. Stunned, I watched as he bolted across the field. He zipped through our patrol line and kept going, howling at something up ahead.

We all crouched on one knee, raised our guns, and

scanned the horizon. Not only were we totally exposed, but now we had a dog calling attention to our position. One of the marines raised his rifle and aimed at Fred. Through my night-vision goggles, I could see the infrared light from his gun illuminate the dog in the dark.

Frantically, I reached into the dirt around me, searching for a stone or clump of soil to throw at Fred to get him to snap out of it and shut up. My fingers only found dust.

Fred kept barking.

With the infrared light shining on Fred, we could see something beyond him that must've been the reason for his barking. In the next field over, I made out a dark wool blanket stretched out across the ground.

I looked over at Ali, who saw it, too. "Let's go," I said, and we moved toward it as the marines fanned out, some with their rifles aimed toward the blanket, others scanning the horizon. Ali and I jogged past Fred, who stood back, growling.

One of the guys grabbed Fred by the scruff to make sure he stayed put. Reaching for a dried cornstalk lying on the ground, he picked it up and used it as a tug-of-war toy to distract the dog.

As Ali and I got closer, it was clear there were people underneath the blanket. Ali shouted for them to come out, and two young men stood up. We separated them for questioning. They claimed to be farmers, showing us the small hand shovels they were carrying. But they couldn't answer any of our simple questions about the fields, like what they were planting or how long they'd worked in the village. It was obvious that they were planting bombs.

We weren't equipped to take prisoners, and they didn't have anything incriminating with them to justify the risk and effort to detain them. We took their pictures and released them.

I worried that the Taliban knew about our night patrols and were keeping track of our movements. If they knew we were avoiding paths and cutting through fields, they'd lay their booby traps accordingly. One thing was definitely clear: Fred's time patrolling with us was over. I couldn't have him putting us—and himself—in that position again if we were going to survive this mission.

The next night when we lined up at the door to head out, Fred scampered between us as he always did, ready for his nightly outing. As we ducked through our tiny doorway, Top counted us one by one, tapping us on the back as he always did. When I went through the door with Fred at my heels, Top reached down and grabbed him by his scruff. "Not anymore, buddy," he said. "You're on radio duty with me now."

For the rest of our time in Afghanistan, Fred waited in the compound each night with Top, assuming his new position as greeter in chief.

In the Green Zone, irrigation canals cut across the fields, creating a giant maze. Sometimes we'd cross them by placing two long wooden posts side by side and shimmying across like the farmers did; other times we'd wade through the water. When we encountered dry canals, they could be used as pathways. At about five feet deep, they provided great cover, and they were unlikely to be rigged with bombs since they frequently flooded.

One night we were cutting through a dry canal when we spotted people moving above us in an adjacent field. We were shocked. We rarely saw anyone out in the dead of night. Through our night-vision goggles, we watched a military-aged man walking swiftly, followed by five or six young boys. The man carried a pillowcase sack over his shoulder, and the whole crew had the same posture—bent forward as if sneaking around, moving quickly.

We thought they were planting bombs for the Taliban, which routinely used kids to place explosives. On my previous mission, I saw a Taliban fighter drive into a compound on a motorcycle with a young boy sitting in front of him and another sitting behind. Hanging over the side was a bag with a soccer ball inside. Once they entered the compound, they were obscured from sight. Next thing I knew, five kids came bounding out, excitedly kicking the soccer ball between them. As they played, I watched one of the boys from the motorcycle dig a hole using a small garden trowel. He buried a homemade explosive and covered it up. The other boy from the motorcycle carried the pressure plate that would trigger the bomb. He dug another shallow hole and carefully connected it with wires. The whole thing only took a couple of minutes; it was clear they were well trained.

With the job done, the guy on the motorcycle emerged from the compound again. The boys quickly got on, and they drove away. Not only did the Taliban use the kids to do their work and serve as their body armor, but the use of children made it impossible for us to interfere. If we'd shot that Taliban fighter, it would have been in front of a group of young kids who probably viewed him as a good guy, a friend who gave them a soccer ball.

Most bombs were planted at night. Sometimes they were disconnected during the day for the safety of the farmers, and then hooked up at night.

From the canal, we watched the group come closer.

I turned to Ali and the nearest marine to me, and said, "Come on." We ducked into a nearby canal and spread out. The canal was narrow, only about three feet wide, and we moved quickly, trying not to let our gear scrape the sides. The group was ahead of us now, and the canal came right up alongside their path overhead. My heart raced. When we were in position, we jumped up out of the canal and approached them. I grabbed the man by his collar and pulled him into the canal while the other marines gathered the boys.

"WHO ARE YOU?" I shouted.

I pinned him down in the dirt with my knee, bearing down on his chest. I leaned toward his face so he could see my eyes.

"Are you Taliban?" I spat the words, not waiting for an answer.

The man was in his twenties or thirties. He had a black beard and a shaved head. Most of the men we met in Afghanistan grew their hair out then buzzed it off once a year. I could tell he had just shaved his because his scalp was still raw and pink. He wore plastic sandals, a dusty white robe, loose pants, and a tan vest.

Stunned, he was stumbling over his words; eventually gathering speed, he repeated a phrase again and again that I didn't understand. Before Ali could translate, another marine reached down and grabbed me by the shoulder.

"Look at this," he said.

He was pointing to the sack the guy had been carrying. He opened it so I could see inside. Beside him, the kids sat in stunned silence. They were young, between six and nine years old, and they sat huddled together. The whites of their wide, fearful eyes were bright in the moonlight.

I looked inside the bag, expecting to find explosives, wires, and pliers. Instead, it was full of books. Confused, I pulled them out. There were math books, religion books, notebooks, and pencils. School supplies?

I turned back to the man. We looked at each other for a moment. I took my knee off his chest and pulled him up so he could sit. Ali and I brushed the dirt from his back.

"I'm a teacher," he was saying in Pashto, tears in his eyes. "A schoolteacher."

I had never heard the word *teacher* in Pashto before.

"I'm so sorry," I said, stunned. "We thought you were Taliban."

Ali and another marine helped the kids down into the canal for cover, and we sat and talked.

"You're a teacher?" I asked. Ali began to translate his words. The man told us his name was Asif. He and his older brother had created a makeshift schoolhouse in a compound in the nearby village. It was just a small room tucked away in a house. At night, Asif and his brother would make their way through the surrounding villages and gather children, bringing them back to the schoolhouse to teach them under the dim light of an oil lamp. They had to hide because the Taliban prohibited any form of education. No books. No music. No writing. No school.

"If the Taliban find out, they will kill me," Asif said. "Like they killed my brother."

About a month ago, Asif said, the Taliban found out what he and his brother were doing. They captured both brothers and forced them onto their knees side by side. They shot his brother and left Asif to bear the message.

I looked over at the kids, who were still sitting quietly, watching us. They hadn't said a word the entire time. I doubt they'd ever interacted with someone from the military before. They looked terrified and small.

I tried to find out about Asif's brother's killers, but Asif didn't know much. He remembered four or five men but didn't know who they were. After the night of his brother's death, he'd never seen them again.

Between the damp walls of the canal, everything smelled like earth. The sky above was dark and still.

I told Asif it was dangerous to move around in the fields with the kids. "We could have shot you," I said.

He looked at me. His eyes had dried, and his voice was calm and measured. "I'm not going to stop teaching," he said. "Whether you kill me or the Taliban do."

My eyes met his, and I understood there was nothing I could say that would convince him to change his ways.

"Please, just stay in one place, at least for tonight," I pleaded. He pointed to a village nearby, saying they weren't going much farther.

We helped Asif and the boys climb out of the canal, and we returned their things. As they continued through the night, the books slung over Asif's shoulders, the patrol watched them until they reached their destination.

Back at the compound, as I lay with Fred on my mat, I couldn't stop thinking about the schoolteacher, his brother, and the children huddled in the ditch. Our mission was to beat back the Taliban, clear the bombs, make the area safe, and, hopefully, supply the area with electricity. I thought of all the money and resources—and weapons—that were being poured into the country. Was that really what those kids needed from us?

Each day, from sunup to sundown, Taliban bullets and bombs crashed in and around our compound. But I felt the threat of the Taliban most deeply when I met people like Asif. He had every right to give up and retreat into despair, anger, and fear. Instead of quitting in the midst of the horror, he stood up and pledged to make the world better.

On one particularly hot day, Fred and I took refuge from the sun under a tarp. Afghanistan's afternoon heat could be brutal, and this was one of the worst heat waves yet. Under the tarp, I wiped the sweat from my forehead and finished up a report while Fred snoozed nearby. As I typed my notes, I saw one of the Afghan soldiers working with the marines pacing around the compound. The commandos or soldiers from the Afghan National Army had been embedded with us to help communicate with the villagers and contribute to our mission. Jason, a British Royal Marine, was training them.

Sometimes, the commandos were a wonderful resource. They understood the culture and helped us connect with the villagers. In my previous assignment, we worked with a group of Afghan guys who patrolled with us. One of them, a teenager named Ali, volunteered to be an interpreter when our Ali needed a break. He was a talented, hardworking kid who had learned English from watching bootleg American movies.

In Sangin, the Afghan soldiers had a different attitude.

From the start, they disagreed with our approach of patrolling at night. They thought it was risky, so they refused to join us. Since most of the mission involved the night patrols, the commandos spent the majority of their days inside the compound, bored.

One Afghan commando did nothing but complain. After seeing one of us feed Fred, he asked, "How can you marines expect respect when you treat this disgusting dog like he is a person?"

Usually, we ignored him. We understood that taking care of Fred probably seemed strange. From the Afghan point of view, it didn't make sense to use resources on pets.

The commando looked irritated. He wore a dark green camouflage uniform and heavy boots as he huffed around the compound, kicking up dirt. Fred, who was having a tough time staying cool under the tarp, got up and walked toward a shady spot under the bushes. As I watched their paths cross, I held my breath. The commando pulled back his right leg and kicked Fred in the rib cage. The force knocked Fred sideways. He let out a loud whimper and spun around.

Before I could react, another marine jumped up and got in the commando's face. That marine, Dave, was a tough guy from Michigan with a MADE IN DETROIT tattoo across his wrist. When it came to

Fred, Dave was a softy. I'd often catch him looking for Fred or calling him over to give him a treat.

"Kick that dog again and I'll bury you out here," Dave said, his voice tight but steady.

The Afghan commando wasn't afraid. He'd been looking for entertainment, and now he had someone's attention.

"He's a filthy dog," he said. "I kick this dog if I want to! Forget you!"

The afternoons in Afghanistan were always hot, but on this particular afternoon, the heat was more intense than usual. The day had been quiet and oppressive, with no activity from the Taliban. It was like everyone in the desert was suffocating.

The commando raised his foot, getting ready to kick Fred again. Dave swiftly brought his own foot up, kicking the sole of his boot directly into the soldier's chest. The commando fell backward into the dirt.

A crowd gathered. As the other Afghan guys walked over, I was shocked to see their weapons in their arms. The commando got up, and the group stood around him, holding their guns.

Across from them, the marines picked up their weapons and faced off. I got to my feet and looked around. Our beards were caked in dirt and our skin had darkened, brown from the sun and the dust. We looked emaciated. Between the lousy food and the constant anxiety, we'd all dropped ten or fifteen pounds. We were angry. Exhausted.

Then I looked down at Fred, who was at Dave's heels. He stood there, panting in the heat, his tail tucked down, confused.

The commando brushed himself off and looked from Dave to Fred. With a bitterness that knocked the air from my lungs, he said, "I'm going to shoot this dog."

He reached for a gun from the hands of the guy next to him.

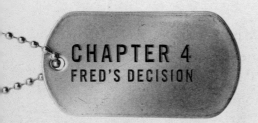

CHAPTER 4
FRED'S DECISION

THE MARINES AND THE AFGHAN commandos stood across from one another, sweaty and squinting in the sun, guns in their arms.

"Stand down," said Jason, the Royal Marine in charge of the Afghan forces, as he stepped into the middle of the group. "Drop your weapons or you can expect your pay to be withheld."

The threat of losing pay ended the standoff quickly. Jason walked up to the commando who had kicked Fred and grabbed the weapon out of his hands. With that, he and the rest of the commandos shuffled through the dust back to their side of the compound, and I followed a few of the marines into the command center, Fred at my heels.

The atmosphere in the compound was uneasy, to say the least. The fact that we had gotten anywhere close to engaging in a gunfight with the commandos was unacceptable. We were nearing the end of our mission, and everyone's nerves were shot. We looked and felt terrible. Hiking for miles each night—never knowing if the next step would be our last—left us exhausted.

We squatted on dusty mats and stained pillows in the command center, sweating. Someone passed around vacuum-sealed fudge brownies.

"We need to come up with a Fred watch," Jason said. "We need to agree that we'll be accountable for him, especially at night. We gotta keep him away from the commandos. If he bothers them or gets in their way, it might force their hand." The commandos had a room at the other side of the compound where they slept. We didn't want Fred wandering over there while we were out on patrols. We all agreed to keep a closer watch on the dog.

But what was really on our minds was a much bigger question: what would happen to Fred when we left? In about a week we were leaving for a two-week break the same way we'd come in: by helicopter in the middle of the night. No one wanted Fred to stay behind.

He'd become one of us. For the past three weeks, he'd lived in the dirt with us, patrolled with us, comforted us, and given us something to smile about, without asking anything in return.

Fred wasn't like other strays in Afghanistan. I couldn't picture him joining a pack of those huge howling dogs, roaming through the Green Zone at night, barking and fighting over food. And after witnessing Fred getting kicked, the threat of human cruelty loomed in my mind, too.

While all the marines had grown attached to Fred, any responsibility for him fell with me. All the guys knew—and I knew, too—that Fred was my dog. He followed me around, slept on my mat, and kept an eye on me more than on anyone else. I knew we had a special bond from the moment I handed him a piece of jerky that first day. So as the final days of our mission slipped by, the pressure mounted for me to figure out how to get Fred out.

There were several challenges. First, there was the issue of sneaking the dog onto the helicopter and smuggling him back to Camp Leatherneck, the large military base where we were going to stay between missions. Second, I had to figure out a way to ship him back to the United States—a huge logistical challenge I didn't even know how to begin to tackle. And third, while I was figuring out how to get Fred to the United States, I would have to keep him hidden at Camp Leatherneck, a place where, if caught, he would be put down immediately.

Camp Leatherneck was huge—1,600 acres—home to the largest number of coalition troops in Afghanistan. And many of the marines were high ranking, with nothing better to do than report a sergeant with a dog in his room.

I could only imagine the consequences I might face if I got caught with a dog—anything from removal from operations to time in the brig, the military prison. Everyone knew there was an order from the commanding general of all US forces in Afghanistan: no pets.

Worst of all, if we got caught, Fred would be euthanized—put to death—immediately, no questions asked. I would have effectively killed him by removing him from his natural environment. How could I risk that? Instead of endangering both of our lives, I wondered if I should just snap some pictures of my furry friend and keep them as a pleasant memory.

Around the compound, the guys tried to help. Plenty of them had stories. "I heard about a guy in Iraq who used this organization called Baghdad Pups," said one marine. Someone else thought he had heard of a humane society back home that raised money to get a dog out. Those were nice suggestions, but we didn't have that kind of time. Plus, in every dog story I'd ever heard, the dog in question had been hanging around a base for months until someone took steps to figure out the paperwork to send the dog home. In our case, we were *taking* Fred from the compound where we'd found him—against orders—and bringing him to a military base where he wasn't allowed to be.

Matt and Dave, a couple of guys I'd spent a lot of time with, wanted to help. They worked with the explosives, and on Leatherneck their unit had a separate section of the base. "It'll be fine," Dave said. "We'll figure it out."

Since Top was in leadership, he couldn't promise anything. But he did say he'd pass around a hat back on base and round up donations to go toward the cost of shipping Fred home.

"You're gonna figure it out," the guys would say. "You can do it, Grossi."

I knew the guys meant what they said. I knew they'd help me. But I also took their promises with a grain of salt. Back on base, people spend their time calling home, hitting the gym, doing office work, and reconnecting with buddies. We'd all go our separate ways for a while, taking space, resting. Friends looking after Fred would not only have the hassle of hiding him, they'd also be putting their careers on the line. I trusted the guys, but I also knew someone had to take responsibility for Fred, and that was me. *If I do this*, I thought, *I'm on my own.*

As the sun went down on the day we were leaving, the marines on the rooftop positions pulled out their knives and slashed open the sandbags in front of them. The bags sagged, weeping sand and dust. Down below, we rolled up our sleeping mats and bug nets, collected our weapons, rounded up our iPods and beat-up copies of old magazines, and loaded everything into our backpacks. The burn pit, which was always smoldering, burned the wrappers and waste. The black smoke billowed into the sky.

Bringing a helicopter down in a combat zone is a huge risk. One well-placed grenade and—*BOOM!*— there goes the whole platoon. Getting out was going to be one of the riskiest parts of our mission. There was no way we could do it from our current compound. The Taliban knew exactly where we were. The plan was to break down the base in the middle of the night, hike to a compound a few miles away, and get picked up in the dark, undetected.

Earlier that day, while gathering my belongings, I spent time with Fred. I gave him his favorite beef jerky and his dusty tug-of-war rope. I'd already taken pictures of him, but I realized I didn't have any of us together. Before I packed up my camera, I handed it to one of the guys and pulled Fred onto my lap for a photo. In the picture, my face is turned toward the shutter but Fred is looking at the rope in my hand, his front paws reaching toward it. The tip of his pink tongue hangs from his snout, and he has the expression of a puppy focused on his favorite toy. After the photo was taken, we played a little longer, and I scratched him behind the ears and massaged his neck. It was as close to a goodbye as I'd let myself get.

I wasn't sure what to do about Fred. I knew I wanted to bring him home, but I could only take the risk if I knew Fred wanted to come, too. If he seemed content staying in his compound—the only home he'd known—then I'd accept it as the best thing for him. It had to be his choice.

With all of us working, it didn't take long before the compound returned to the state we'd found it in when we arrived. We left nothing behind. Our makeshift home would soon be crawling with Taliban, and we didn't leave anything they could use.

Loaded with gear, we lined up by the back door. I saw Fred poking around the burn pit looking for scraps. The guys got quiet as we got ready to head out, and I focused on the journey ahead. When the first marine pushed through the doorway, we followed him into the night, single file, the same way we'd come.

The desert was cool and clear with a sliver of moon overhead. Through my night-vision, I looked at the sloping sand hills rolling softly in the distance. The open landscape was a welcome change from the dense cornfields and network of canals in the Green Zone. I felt like I could see for miles in every direction—but I didn't see Fred. I had wanted him to make the decision for me, and now he had. I told myself I should accept it, but I was heartbroken.

Several hours later, miles from our compound, we approached another compound, which had been located by drone. It was smaller and full of goats—a good sign there wasn't a network of bombs underfoot. We filed in, and a few marines scouted from the rooftop. The rest of us kept a low profile. It was almost morning. Once light broke, we'd spend the day waiting for dark to return and, with it, our ride out of there.

For the first time in weeks, I felt the weight of the mission begin to lift. I didn't have any reports to write. There were no villagers to talk to. We were getting out—and we were getting out with all our guys. That felt like nothing short of a miracle. The bullet that passed through Joe's helmet on the first day had been the closest we had come to losing someone. We were lucky. Now, we could rest.

As the morning sun peeked over the horizon, I sat down and leaned onto my backpack, finally allowing myself to think about a shower and hot meal rather than how much I missed Fred. I stretched my legs out in front of me and crossed my arms on my chest, resting my head back against the wall and closing my eyes.

I awoke to shouts from the guys on the roof. "Grossi! Get up here!"

Daylight had broken across the new compound. I blinked my eyes open and saw the guys sitting in the shade along the perimeter walls. Confused, I got to my feet and wandered over to a rickety wooden ladder. I climbed onto the roof and someone handed me binoculars.

"Look who it is," he said.

The desert, glowing and hazy in the morning sun, looked out of focus. There were miles of nothing and then, coming toward us, a squatty white dog trailed by a cloud of dust. Goose bumps rose on my arms. It was Fred, the sun in his eyes, bounding toward us with that signature bounce in his step, chin up.

"Dude must've needed to pack!" The guys laughed.

I blinked away the sting of tears. I couldn't believe it.

"Good boy," I whispered.

Fred pranced right through the doorway of the compound like he owned the place. In typical Fred fashion, he greeted each marine one at a time, howling and *woo-wooing*, dancing between us with joy. I came down from the roof and grabbed a piece of beef jerky. When Fred frolicked over to me, I swear he was smiling. He wound through my legs in excitement, as if to say, "Where'd you go?"

I squatted to give him the jerky, then pulled out my collapsible coffee cup and poured him some water. As he lapped it up, I shook my head in disbelief. Had he spent the night scavenging through the burn pit? Was he waiting for the sun to come up before following us? I wasn't sure how he did it, but Fred had tracked us down.

After sunrise, the temperature spiked, as it always did. Fred, entertained by the goats, chased them from one corner of the compound to another. He trotted over, lowering his head to the ground to nip at their wobbly ankles. They squealed and dashed away as he followed. We sat around in the shade watching and laughing. We were still stunned and excited that Fred had followed us. But if I was going to get him out of the field completely, there was still the issue of how, exactly, I'd get him on the helicopter.

We tried to figure out what to do.

"What if we just walk him onto the helicopter like he's a working dog?" Jason suggested. Back at the compound, Jason had made Fred a collar and leash, using a button and some cord. Fred hated the thing and managed to wriggle free each time we put it on him.

"There's no way we'll get away with that," I said. "They know we didn't come here with a dog. We can't just stroll onto the helicopter with one when we leave."

"What if we just hide Fred in our gear?" someone suggested. In the field, we all carried thin, foldable duffel bags. If a fellow marine was injured in action, you'd use the bag to gather the guy's equipment so nothing was left behind. We got out a duffel bag and tried to see how Fred would react to being put inside it. Two guys held the bag open while I lifted Fred by the torso and placed him inside. As soon as he hit the ground, he threw his head back, squirmed out, and bolted away. Tail wagging, he came back and looked at us, as if to say, "Try it again!" He thought it was a game.

Jim, the corpsman who had helped remove Fred's bugs, had a better idea. "I can give him Benadryl. It'll knock him out, then you can put him right in and he won't know the difference."

I figured that was worth a shot. Jim stuck the little pink pill on the back of Fred's tongue and closed his hands around his snout until Fred swallowed. Fred settled down and closed his eyes, but it was hard to tell if it was the Benadryl or if Fred just got tired and decided to take a nap.

We sat in the shade, Fred sleeping next to me, and the guys took turns coming over to ask if I had a plan. "Grossi, you gotta do it, man," they pressed.

"Relax," I said. "I'm working on it."

It wasn't long before Fred was up and poking around the compound again. With the marines off my back for a minute, I decided to make a deal with Fred. Gently, I pulled him toward me.

"Okay, buddy," I said, looking into his light brown eyes. "If you really want to get out of here, you're gonna have to show me one more thing. Okay?"

I told myself and I told Fred that if he followed me toward the helicopter when it came—if he wasn't afraid of the noise and the dust—then I'd take him with me. I still wasn't sure if what I was doing was right. I didn't want to steal this dog, and I didn't want to put him or anyone else in danger. To go through with it, I needed one last sign.

I stuffed my duffel bag into my cargo pocket so it'd be easy to reach. If Fred came with me, one way or another I'd get him inside that bag.

I made a call to my commanding officer back at Camp Leatherneck. He was a good boss, and I trusted him. I wanted his advice. "I might be bringing a dog back with me," I said.

I don't remember if he laughed or sighed. "I'm not gonna tell you that you can't," he said. "But if you get caught, you're on your own."

That was probably the best outcome I could have hoped for. I asked him to pass the phone to Sergio, one of my close buddies at Camp Leatherneck. Sergio was a smart, fast-talking Puerto Rican–Italian guy who wore thick glasses. He was so smart that he had trouble communicating with the rest of us; we couldn't keep up. He also had the biggest heart of anyone I'd met in the marines. I knew I could trust Sergio to help.

On Camp Leatherneck, we had access to a few pickup trucks that we used to get to and from meetings across base. If someone could bring one of those trucks to meet us when we landed, we could whisk Fred away before anyone realized what was going on.

"Hey, man," I said when Sergio came on the line. "I need you to bring the truck to the flight line when we land. I might have a dog with me."

Sergio didn't hesitate before promising to be there with another friend, Mac, a radio guy from Wyoming. Mac was an Iraq veteran and a solid marine with a great sense of humor. He was eager to get out of Camp Leatherneck on a mission, but most of the marines had their own radio operators, so Mac was stuck back at the base in an office with Sergio.

Next, I called my big sister, Sarah, back in Virginia. In her work as a special education teacher and school counselor, she'd seen her way around tough situations. But she always kept a cool head and wasn't afraid to take action.

I told her about Fred. I also briefed her on the risks and how much trouble I'd be in if I got caught. Sarah was unfazed and a step ahead of me. I'd mentioned Fred to Sarah during a call a couple weeks back. She'd already been emailing a few organizations to get an idea of how we'd be able to get Fred back to the United States and through customs.

"Oh, hush," she said. "If anyone can do it, it's you, Craig. If you get him out of the field, I'll take care of the rest."

The calls gave me hope, but they didn't calm my nerves.

As the time of our departure approached, I paced the compound, checking my gear, checking on Fred, thinking and worrying. We got a call telling us that the helicopters would be there eight hours later than expected. Instead of picking us up in the middle of the night, the helicopters would come at daybreak.

This was unsettling news. The Taliban had recently

shot down a helicopter. If we left in the light of day, would the same thing happen to us? If I was having a tough time getting Fred into the duffel bag, that delay in our departure could be critical. As much as I loved Fred, this wasn't a game, and when it came to it, I knew I wasn't going to risk the lives of marines for the sake of a dog.

I didn't sleep much that night. In the morning, everyone was quiet as we packed up. Three helicopters were coming in, and I'd be on the first one. We assembled along the wall, and I stood toward the back of the line. The guys were jittery, shifting from foot to foot. Fred, sensing something was about to happen, bopped around, looking at us with anticipation. Gazing at Fred, I felt a tightness in my chest. This might be it.

The low thump of the rotors in the distance broke the morning quiet. The helicopters we used to get in and out of the field were huge. Two would land and load while the third hovered for cover. Once the first two were back in the air, the third would come down for the last of the guys.

As the first giant helicopter landed outside the compound wall, a wave of sand and dust covered us like a fog. It was a brownout. A helicopter always kicks up a wave of dust, but it usually washes over and clears. But sometimes the dust lingers, making a relatively simple thing—boarding the helicopter—complicated and dangerous. With poor visibility, marines have been killed in brownouts by accidentally running into tail rotors.

We were about to leave. Fred paced nervously. The line moved forward, and I ducked through the doorway of the compound. Dust and rocks pelted my body. I coughed and squinted, stepping through the brown cloud toward the deafening sound of the whirring rotors. All I could see was the backpack of the marine ahead of me, but no Fred.

I moved forward and felt a poke at my heel. I looked through the grit and grime and saw Fred looking up at me. He was barely able to open his eyes. His ears were pinned back, and he looked terrified. But there it was. My sign.

Without thinking, I pulled the duffel bag from my cargo pocket. From behind me, Top's hand emerged through the dust and clutched Fred by the scruff. He lifted him like a jug of milk.

"We're doing this!" Top shouted. In one fluid motion, I yanked open the mouth of the bag and Top dropped Fred inside. I zipped it, and we each picked it up by a handle, rushing forward.

A young air winger stood at the back of the chopper, rifle up, scanning the horizon and watching us board. He looked at Top and me, lowered his gaze to the bag between us, and scowled. He reached his arm out to stop us, parting his lips to say something, but Top lifted his forearm, elbow bent, and blocked him.

"Don't worry about it!" Top barked, and we stepped up onto the ramp.

We were the last to board. As soon as we were inside, the air winger ducked in behind us, resuming his position on the ramp, and the helicopter lifted back into the air.

I sat on the floor, leaning back into my pack with Fred in the duffel between my legs. My fellow marines looked at me with huge grins. Top extended his arm for a congratulatory fist bump.

I pressed my palms onto Fred's back, through the bag, trying to let him know he was okay. I could only imagine how afraid he must have been. Here was a dog who had never even ridden in a car before, and now he was flying through the air in a helicopter. I felt him squirm, trying to get comfortable, then settle.

"Good boy," I whispered.

As we soared through the morning sky, I realized that this scrappy, short-legged, dusty dog was officially mine now. He'd put his trust in me. The real challenge still lay before us, but I was resolved. My sister was right: if there was a person to do this, it was me. I'd have to find a way.

CHAPTER 5
OPERATION FRED

WHEN THE HELICOPTER touched down at Camp Leatherneck, I lifted the duffel bag with Fred inside and tucked it under my arm. As I walked across the airfield, I felt like I was stepping on land for the first time after a month at sea. The sun was bright overhead, and the wind from the rotors shook loose a cloud of dust from our uniforms.

There was a welcome-back reception for us right there on the airfield, complete with pizza and cold Gatorade. I hadn't had a cold drink in weeks, but I was going to have to wait a little longer. With my four-legged stowaway in my bag, I slipped away from the guys and walked toward the road where I planned to meet Sergio.

I knelt behind a barrier of dirt-filled barrels and looked anxiously into the distance. Fred squirmed inside the bag. I opened the zipper and let him pop his head out. He lifted his snout toward the sky and sniffed the air, then scanned his surroundings, panting and blinking under the hot sun.

When I arrived at Camp Leatherneck for the first time several months earlier, the size of the base shocked me. It was big enough to drive around and get lost. There were three dining halls, four state-of-the-art gyms, a hospital, clinics, a post office, and row after row of office buildings, tents, and barracks. There was a huge internet lounge, a place where soldiers could get a cup of coffee and play video games. Camp Bastion, the British-run base with an airfield, was connected to Camp Leatherneck, too. That was where the helicopters and drones went in and out.

At Camp Leatherneck, I felt safe. I saw civilian contractors walking from building to building and marines driving around in civilian vehicles. A lot of marines spent their entire deployment at Camp Leatherneck. Those who worked in supply and some intelligence analysts stayed on base. Every job was important, but I was grateful to have spent as much time in the field as I did.

Fred waited quietly. Finally, a little black Toyota pickup came down the dirt road, kicking up a dusty cloud in its wake. As the Toyota came closer, I spotted Sergio behind the wheel and Mac sitting beside him, with his oversized cowboy grin. They pulled up next to my hiding spot, and I zipped Fred back into the duffel bag and put him in the bed of the truck. I jumped in beside him. The diesel engine let out a groan as Sergio shifted gears, and we lurched forward, speeding toward our barracks on the opposite side of the base.

As we drove, I opened the duffel bag and let Fred out. He struggled to keep his balance as we bounced down the road.

"You look like hell, man!" Sergio shouted from the cab, grinning and handing me a bottle of water. I took a swig and was shocked by how strange it felt to drink something cold. I found a plastic cup rolling around in the back of the truck and poured some water for Fred.

Camp Leatherneck was always expanding and changing. As we drove toward the barracks, I spotted a new compound off to the side of the road that hadn't been there when I left a month ago. In bright red letters against a yellow background, a small sign near its entrance read DHL, the international shipping service.

Sergio pulled up to our barracks. The long white trailers were lined with bunks and slept about ten guys each. No one else was there, which worked in Fred's favor.

I plopped Fred down on my bunk.

"Hey, Freddy, here's your first bed," I said. Impressed, the dusty dog curled up right there, blinking his eyes sleepily and letting out a sigh.

Sergio, Mac, and I laughed at him. After talking for a few minutes, Mac said, "Hey, man, go get a shower. We'll stay with the little guy."

In the shower, the water felt amazing. I turned it as hot as it would go and stood under the faucet, letting the pressure rinse the sand from my hair. Brown water pooled at my feet. Afterward, I shaved and put on fresh clothes. The pants were so clean they felt stiff and foreign against my body.

We spent the rest of the afternoon camped out in the barracks with Fred. Mac brought us some food from the dining hall, and we watched movies on my laptop. I found some rope and planned to use it as a leash for Fred. Once it was good and dark, Mac kept a lookout while I took the dog outside for a walk.

The night was clear and cool. Our barracks was at the end of the row, so we didn't have to go far to reach a field that was fairly secluded. Not many people drove around at night. Fred was calm; he didn't struggle against the leash or make a sound. In the dark, his white fur seemed to almost glow against the moon-dusted earth. I watched as he sniffed around, nose to the ground, finding places to mark. Once he was done, we went back inside. Fred seemed to understand what was happening, so he was especially cooperative.

That night, lying in bed with Fred between my knees, I was too anxious to sleep. I would be going back to Sangin after a two-week break on base. I needed to get Fred out before going back into the field.

I thought about the DHL sign I had seen. The shipping company had likely popped up to meet the growing shipping demands on Camp Leatherneck. We had a military post office to handle troop mail and care packages. DHL was a civilian company. Instead of military staff, they'd have their own workers. Getting civilians to help me with Fred seemed safer than involving other marines. The place was crawling with military police, but the civilian-run contractor buildings were off the radar. If Fred was going to get shipped home, DHL would be his ticket out.

The next morning, with Fred hidden back at the barracks, I went over to the DHL compound. A twelve-foot chain-link fence surrounded the area. I walked up to the gate, which was closed but not locked. I pushed it open just enough to squeeze through.

The place looked abandoned. A forklift was parked just inside the gate. In the back, a few trailers sat quietly. Propped up against one of them, I spotted a small yellow sign that read OFFICE in red letters.

I tapped on the door, and it swung open. Inside was a cheap, wobbly-looking desk with a computer monitor and keyboard. From underneath it, I heard a man with what I thought was a thick Ugandan accent. "Come in!" he said as he lifted his hand and waved me inside.

The DHL worker picked himself up off the floor with a groan and wiped his forehead with a white towel. Without looking at me, he pressed his index finger against the power button—tapping repeatedly—until the computer whirred to life. A satisfied smile on his face, he finally turned to me.

"Yes, Sergeant. What can I do for you?" he said.

"Please, call me Craig," I told him.

The man smiled and nodded as he came around the desk with his hand outstretched.

"Okay, Craig. My name is Tinashe. It is nice to meet you. And what can I do for you?"

Tinashe was about five foot eight and in his forties. He was bald and clean-shaven. With his blue DHL polo shirt tucked into his belted khakis, he looked sharp, and he smiled generously.

"I'm thinking of shipping something, but it looks

like you guys aren't quite up and running yet," I said, scanning the room.

Tinashe smiled even bigger and said, "Oh, don't worry, my friend! We'll be up and running within twenty-four hours. Things move quickly here; I make sure of that. What were you thinking of shipping?"

I took a quick breath and tried to sound smooth. "If someone had a dog—hypothetically—would that be something you could ship?"

Tinashe looked at me, still smiling. "How big is this dog?" he asked, crossing his arms across his chest.

"Oh, I'm just curious if—," I started to say, but Tinashe, laughing, cut me off.

"Bring him over! I want to meet this dog!" he said.

"Okay, man," I said. "I'll bring him over here tomorrow."

"I can't make any promises but I will promise you I'll do what I can," he said.

First thing the following morning, I snuck Fred into the pickup, making him ride on the floor of the passenger side. We drove toward DHL, cautiously passing by a military police vehicle parked outside the dining hall.

When we pulled up to the DHL compound, I was shocked. It had been transformed. The forklift operator lifted a pallet of water bottles onto a flatbed truck. Tinashe stood, wearing the same blue polo, clipboard in hand, giving orders to workers as they zipped around. When he saw me, he waved me over to a parking spot by the office.

Fred popped up onto the passenger seat, and when Tinashe got a look at him, his face lit up. He went over to Fred's side and opened the door for him.

"Look at this funny guy! You didn't tell me he was such a good-looking dog!" Tinashe said as Fred spilled out onto the dusty ground, excitedly prancing around Tinashe's feet.

We walked into the office and Tinashe handed me a printout.

"That is a list of forms that you'll need to get this guy home," he said, bending to rub Fred behind the ears. "What is his name, by the way?"

"Oh, I'm sorry—this is Fred," I said.

Tinashe burst out in laughter.

"Fred!" he said. "Fred the Afghan with the American friend!"

I couldn't help but laugh, too. A couple of the DHL workers wandered in to see what all the excitement was about. One of them introduced himself as Peter; he was in Afghanistan to make some cash and send it to his family in the Philippines. He said most of his coworkers were Filipino, too. Well-paying jobs in the Philippines were hard to come by, and Peter had traveled half a world away to support his loved ones. Most overseas military bases I have seen are staffed by third country nationals. They are people from one country—such as the Philippines—working in another country—such as Afghanistan—for a company from a third country— such as DHL. I respected the sacrifices these people were making to survive and support their families back home.

Tinashe pointed to a huge chart on the wall. It was a long list of things they weren't permitted to ship— mostly obvious stuff like grenades, rifles, bullets, spent ammunition.

"There's nothing here about live animals, my friend," he said.

I thanked him, and Fred and I made our way back to the barracks.

In the room, I looked at the paperwork, and my heart sank. The list of required forms was long, including papers that sounded nearly impossible for me to obtain, such as customs forms and veterinary certifications, one of which required proof of a rabies vaccination and a thirty-day quarantine supervised by a veterinarian. How was I going to get that?

I pulled out my phone and called Sarah, but she didn't pick up. Rambling nervously, I left a long voice mail describing each of the forms I needed, asking her to find out if she could get her hands on them and mail them to me.

I looked at Fred, sitting on the bed. He looked back at me with raised eyebrows as if asking, "What now?"

Over the next few days, I corresponded with Sarah, who was trying to find out what needed to be done to get an animal shipped from Afghanistan to the United States.

Meanwhile, hiding Fred in the barracks was becoming increasingly stressful. I heard rumors of room inspections. First Sergeants and other higher ups were looking for alcohol and other illegal items, as well as making sure our rooms were clean. Under normal circumstances it would have annoyed me—we weren't in boot camp anymore—but with Fred in our room, I was terrified. There were no locks on the door. Anyone could come in at any time.

After a few days of hiding Fred, I thought I was going to get caught. I went over to the part of the compound where my friends who worked with explosives lived, and my friends Matt and Dave agreed to help hide him. Their compound was farther from most of the activity in Camp Leatherneck, and their commander was a bit more relaxed. We all agreed it would be easier for Fred to stay there, and I drove him over that night.

The next time I talked to Sarah, it was clear that

shipping Fred was going to be trickier than expected. She didn't have any of the forms yet, and we needed extra time to mail them. The days were slipping by. I realized I had to shift my focus from sending Fred home to finding a way to keep him safe while I went out on my next mission. I hated the thought of leaving him on Camp Leatherneck without me, but I didn't have any other choice.

The safest place at Camp Leatherneck would be with civilians. If Fred stayed with the marines, it was only a matter of time until he would be found. In addition, Dave and Matt were finishing their deployment and going home. I had to ask Tinashe if he could hide Fred at the DHL compound.

At dusk, I put Fred in the truck and we drove to DHL. The setting sun and desert haze turned the sky yellow in its last burst of daylight. When we pulled up to the compound, Fred and I hopped out and met Tinashe in the office.

The words came tumbling out.

"Tinashe, I've got a problem. I'm going back out in another week. I'll be gone for a while—like a month—and I don't know what I'm going to do with Fred. We've been trying to hide him, but if we get caught, he'll be put down," I said. "My sister is working on the customs forms but she needs more time. . . ."

Tinashe placed his hand on my shoulder. "My friend, didn't I tell you I would do what I could? Fred will stay here with me while you are gone. This is a special dog, and I want to do my part to make sure he gets to America."

I hugged him.

Tinashe walked outside and moved like a hummingbird, quickly putting together a plan. He picked up a long strap. "Here," he said, tying it to a metal pole. "While we're working all day, Fred can stay here."

Peter and a few of the guys appeared. It was the end of the day and they were off the clock. Several simmering slow cookers sat on a folding table at the back of the office. It was dinnertime, so after hearing the news about Fred, they brought him a plate of chicken and rice.

We were from different countries—separate continents—yet we had been brought together by this one little mutt in the middle of the Afghanistan desert. We were all transplants here, trying to survive in our strange circumstances. These guys didn't have to help me, but they did. I was humbled by their generosity.

As I slipped out and drove away from the compound, Fred barely noticed. He had made new friends, and he was happy.

My two weeks at Camp Leatherneck flew past. In addition to getting Fred settled, I had to prep for the next mission, spending hours in the intelligence office with Sergio while he briefed me on what to expect from the Taliban next time out.

The plan was for us to return a few miles north of where we'd been before, continuing to remove the Taliban along Highway 611. Our goal was to establish a patrol base that would serve as a semipermanent fixture along the highway and secure the area so the engineers could continue to make their way toward the dam.

The farther north we went, the narrower the Green Zone became, cut off by an eastward bend in the Helmand River. This area of the Green Zone was dense with Taliban. From our experience in Sangin, we could tell that the Taliban had been coming down from this area to attack us during the day, then retreating at night. After we left, we monitored the area by drone and saw the Taliban move around completely at ease, unafraid. It was almost as if we'd never been there.

On this mission I was heading out with Ali, the interpreter, as well as two new explosives experts, Justin and Ysa. We met the night we were heading out. Justin was about my height, a big guy, in shape, with huge hands. He had a quiet confidence about him. I knew he was a staff sergeant, but he introduced himself by his first name.

"You're the guy who snuck the dog out in a duffel bag last time out, right?" Justin said.

Someone must have told him about Operation Fred.

"Dude, you're from Pittsburgh, aren't you?" I asked, changing the subject. "I'd recognize that accent anywhere, you freaking yinzer."

Justin immediately smiled. I told him my dad's side of the family was from a small town outside of Pittsburgh. Every time my dad said *house*, it sounded like *hass*. I hadn't heard the western-Pennsylvanian accent in a while but I still had an ear for it.

I also busted Ysa about his name. "Y-S-A?" I said, pronouncing it *why-essay* in a goofy tone. Ysa—which is actually pronounced *ee-ssa*—was, like Justin, easygoing. He was a little shorter than Justin and from a small town in Texas, but his personality was as big as the state itself.

"Look, guys," I said. "The Recon guys are great, but they're their own unit. We should stick together." Justin and Ysa had more combat experience than I did, but this would be their first time in Sangin. We needed one another.

We lugged our gear over so we could load up on the helicopter together. As the sun sank into the dusty horizon, I felt a moment of peace. Fred was safe. I knew

Sarah would find a way to get the forms we needed. I was doing a job I loved, surrounded by a good team of guys.

As the light faded in the sky, we walked across the tarmac and boarded the helicopters, headed back to Sangin. I didn't know it then, but that moment was the quiet before the storm.

CHAPTER 6
BOOM!

WHEN WE ARRIVED, Sangin was eerily quiet. Our new compound sat on the desert side of the highway, in the dusty, moonlike terrain, next to the Green Zone. We got there late at night and waited. When the sun came up, we braced for an attack that didn't come.

After a few days, the Taliban still hadn't launched the kind of assault we'd seen in our earlier mission to Sangin. The Taliban knew where we were—there'd been a few shots fired at our rooftop posts—but we hadn't faced a hard-core attack. We moved forward with our plan to reach out to the villagers and to make our presence known in the Green Zone.

We scheduled the first night patrol. Instead of going out for a few hours then returning, we planned to take over a compound in the Green Zone and stay for forty-eight hours. By securing the compound for a couple of days we'd demonstrate our presence to the locals and the Taliban. We wanted to send a clear message to the Taliban that we were serious and prepared to confront them head-on.

As specialized attachments, Justin, Ysa, and I didn't need to go out with the patrol team. Each patrol had a trained marine who walked in front of the group with a metal detector, sweeping for mines and explosives. If that person found a device that they couldn't handle, they would radio for Justin and Ysa, the experts.

But Justin and Ysa weren't willing to sit back and wait. Their skills were unmatched. They wanted to be on-site when they were needed, not sitting around in the dust waiting for a call.

Ali and I felt the same way. We weren't going to meet any villagers sitting inside the compound. The closer we got to the action, the better intelligence we could gather, whether through watching, talking with families, or interrogating Taliban fighters. We were there to do our jobs the best we could.

That night we lined up and filed out of the compound with the patrol. Earlier that day, we had reviewed the four-mile route down to a village along the river. Drones had spotted a group of Taliban fighters in the area.

After a few weeks off, it felt good to be back on the job. We were used to the challenging terrain now, and we moved swiftly through the Green Zone as a team. Our boots groaned as we marched with a steady rhythm. This part of the Green Zone felt more compact: the plant life was thicker and lusher, and the trees grew taller. Instead of scrawny, naked branches, the plants reached toward the sky, thick with leaves. When we passed villages, I noticed the homes were closer together. Instead of separate buildings, some even shared walls. That made me nervous, since it meant the Taliban could more easily move from one house to another without detection.

We secured a new compound in the Green Zone and planned to hold it for forty-eight hours. Justin, Ysa, and I stayed on watch so that the other marines could rest before the action that we believed would come in the morning. The new compound was small, with a courtyard and breezeway that led to a few rooms. It also had an orchard with pomegranate trees in a separate garden area. The walls around the main compound were at least eight feet high, but around the trees the walls were only about half that height. That arrangement made a good fighting position because we could stand up and shoot over if we needed to, using a couple sandbags to protect our heads.

Under the dark sky, the guys and I leaned against the orchard wall and whispered in the quiet. We had fancy binoculars that operated like our night-vision goggles, and we'd take turns looking through them at the surrounding dirt paths, fields, and compounds. Above us, the machine gunner stood ready on a rooftop post. The night was quiet, and we took off our helmets and relaxed in the cool air.

I told Justin and Ysa about what I'd seen in my previous missions, but mostly we goofed off. Justin and I talked about Pittsburgh, and I teased him about the rivalry between the Penguins and Capitals hockey teams. Justin shut me down by reminding me that my Capitals hadn't won a Stanley Cup—ever.

We swapped stories, talked about where we'd come from and what brought us to Afghanistan. Ysa told us about his high school sweetheart—now his wife—and their three little girls. Justin had us laughing about his adventures and misadventures in high school. I told the guys the story of Fred. As I got to the part about Fred following me to the helicopter, they shook their heads and smiled.

"I can't wait to meet him," Justin said.

"My dog Duchess is gonna want to meet him, too," Ysa added.

After a few hours, the sky began to brighten, and the sun showed up on the horizon. We were off the clock, and we walked from the garden through an archway into the main compound. As we crossed the compound, I spotted something I hadn't seen in Afghanistan outside of Camp Leatherneck: a bed. It wasn't much of a bed—more like a metal frame with plastic bands stretched across it, almost like an oversized pool chair. Still, it looked like a welcome change from sleeping on the ground.

"Dibs!" I yelled, grabbing the bed and pulling it into the breezeway for shade. My boots and pants were still wet from wading through canals, so I took them off, changed into my shorts, and lay back on the little cot. It wasn't quite long enough, but it was good enough. I closed my eyes and started to drift off to the sound of the lieutenant sending radio checks back to the compound where the rest of our unit remained.

That was the last thing I remembered.

A force hit my body like a wave on a beach.

A loud crack.

Darkness.

The memory is murky. I remember seeing a marine's hands reaching through the dust and debris. I remember my body being lifted. I remember hearing my name called.

As the fog cleared, I realized I was now sitting against a wall, across the courtyard from where I'd been sleeping in the cot. Another marine was talking to me: "Craig, buddy. Are you okay?"

I looked back at where I had been sleeping. The ceiling of the breezeway was on fire. Rocks and debris covered the ground. The sound of a firefight buzzed in the air.

What was going on? An explosion. How could it have been so close?

Later, I learned that a Taliban rocket had landed in our compound, directly behind the wall of the breezeway where I was on the cot, causing the whole area to collapse. When the guys looked at where I'd been sleeping and saw the pile of rubble, they thought I had been killed.

"Get your gear on," one of the marines said.

I looked up. The guys were scrambling, getting into position, returning fire.

I suddenly understood: we were under attack.

I found my gear and put on my boots. I tried to pull on my pants, but something was wrong. I struggled to yank my pants over my boots, but they were stuck.

My brain wasn't working right. Instead of taking off

my boots, I took out my knife and cut slits at the bottom of my pants so they'd fit over the boots. I pulled them up and grabbed my gun.

I saw Justin and Ysa and I went to them. *Just do what they do,* I thought.

Everybody was returning fire. The rocket launch had sent a cloud of smoke into the air, so the guys knew their target. There was a pause in the fighting. Then the Taliban opened up on us from another compound, much closer. We switched walls so we could shoot back.

My body and mind were functioning on adrenaline. It was the first time I had been in a battle where the neighboring compounds were so close and we were all on flat ground. We were a small platoon trying to secure a compound in a hornet's nest. We were vulnerable.

The decision was made to call in HIMARS, the High Mobility Artillery Rocket System, which could be fired with precise accuracy from a distance. These rockets were launched from Camp Leatherneck.

The lieutenant sent the coordinates over the radio, and a team back on base fired the rockets. From almost one hundred miles away, the missiles shot into the air, leaving a stream of smoke in their wake. They landed less than 150 feet from us—dangerously close—so we all took cover. Like lightning, the missiles came crashing down around us. The impact of the blasts washed through me like a force, sending painful pulses through my body.

After the blasts, it got quiet. If the Taliban fighters were still alive, they were fleeing. The corner of the compound where the rocket had landed was still smoldering. I took off my gear and helmet and wiped the sweat from my forehead.

The corpsman came over to give me a field exam.

"What's your name?" he asked.

"Craig."

He asked for my mother's name and her maiden name. I answered. Then he asked me how old I was.

"My girlfriend is twenty-eight," I said.

"Okay, but how old are you?"

"I told you," I said. "She's twenty-eight. I'm younger than her."

The corpsman tried again. "Okay. But do you know your age?"

"I just told you!" I shouted, frustrated.

As the adrenaline faded, my head began to throb. The bruise on the back of my skull started to swell. I felt terrible.

The medical specialist had the information he needed: I wasn't okay.

He radioed back to the other compound. "Grossi is

fine but showing signs of head trauma. Potential routine medevac needed later."

I resisted. I'd grown up getting clobbered in ice hockey games. In my mind, I just needed a break—a moment to sit on the bench and shake it off—then I'd be fine. I didn't think it could be that bad. I looked okay. And I didn't want to leave my guys.

Meanwhile, Justin and Ysa poked around at the impact site. They found what was left of a 107mm Chinese anti-tank rocket. It was huge—a few feet long—with the capability of taking out a tank. Afghanistan was littered with rockets like this from the war with the Soviets. The Taliban didn't have a way of accurately firing them, so they would launch the rockets by propping them up with a metal stand and hitting them with a hammer. We'd seen the rockets whizzing by during previous battles, but they were always out of control and off target. We practically laughed at them. I wasn't laughing anymore.

I was in the middle of telling the corpsman I was fine when Justin put the rocket motor in front of me. It was at least a foot long and wider than I could wrap my hand around. At the top end, the metal was warped and twisted from the explosion.

"Look at this," he said. "You can't be as close to this as you were and not be messed up. You gotta get checked out."

He was adamant. In addition to the first blast, the shock waves from the HIMARS could have caused further brain injury.

Instead of having us stay another night and day in the Green Zone, our command decided the whole patrol would hike back to the rest of the company in the desert compound. It was too dangerous for us to stay where we were.

We waited for nightfall, huddled along the wall at one end of the compound. My head pounded. My brain felt too big for my skull. The pressure was miserable. I couldn't eat; I was nauseated. I tried to close my eyes and sleep. I dreamed that a grenade floated over the wall and landed in my lap. I jolted awake, my heart racing.

Once it had been dark for several hours, we left the compound. My balance was off, which made walking difficult. Each time I stepped down into a canal or up onto a bank, I felt like everything was moving sideways. I couldn't use the night-vision goggles, so I took off my helmet and strapped it to my backpack.

Justin was walking behind me. "You okay, man?" he asked.

"Yeah," I said sharply. I hated that the guys were keeping their eyes on me, worrying. I had worked hard to prove myself, to show I was tough, but now I felt like a pile of mashed potatoes.

When we finally reached the compound, I met with the head corpsman, who agreed that I needed to be taken back to Camp Leatherneck.

I argued that I just needed to rest. If they sent me to Leatherneck, would that be the end of my work in Sangin?

Justin and Ysa didn't want to hear it. They helped me pack my stuff while I waited for the helicopter.

"Look, man, you won't be doing anyone any good out here if your brain is bleeding," said Justin.

"Yeah—you don't have the brain cells to spare," Ysa joked, stuffing my sleeping bag into my backpack.

When the helicopter touched down at Camp Leatherneck, my commanding officer, Dave, was waiting for me in the back of an ambulance on the airstrip. We drove to the hospital, and I had to hand over all my gear, including my gun, my knife, and my ammunition. I hated to part with it. What if this was it for me?

At the hospital, the doctor ordered an MRI— magnetic resonance imaging, a procedure that uses a machine to take a detailed picture of what's going on inside the body. After checking out my brain, he sent me to the Battlefield Recovery Center on the base. Reluctantly, I went.

As soon as I walked inside, a wave of air-conditioning

shocked me. The lobby smelled like Otis Spunkmeyer cookies and blueberries. As I stood there, still covered in mud and dirt, I felt as if the ground was moving beneath me. From behind a tall desk, a pretty air force servicewoman was smiling at me; the air force ran the center.

"Hi, there," she said, getting to her feet.

A jar of candy sat on the countertop, and a huge flat-screen TV hung on the wall next to a large stainless steel fridge. Everything was pristine and cold, like a freezer. Suddenly I needed to vomit.

The woman rushed over, followed by two others, and they led me to a bed—a real bed—with clean white sheets. I fell asleep instantly.

I don't know how long I slept, but it must have been a while. I had smeared mud all over the bed. Some brave soul had taken off my boots and put them at the end of my bed. On a chair next to me sat a shave kit with a towel and soap, as well as a fresh uniform. Mac and Sergio must have come by, leaving a bag of beef jerky and a handwritten note: "Clean yourself up, you're filthy. P.S. Glad you're not dead."

I woke up thinking of one thing: Fred.

I took a shower, shaved, and dressed. I didn't feel like myself, but the sleep had helped. An air force officer greeted me. With a clipboard tucked under her arm and a cup of coffee in her hand, she shook my hand, introducing herself as my doctor.

"Is it okay if I ask a few questions?" she asked.

I assumed she had been sent to evaluate me to see if I was fit to continue my deployment. At that point, I was more nervous about Fred than anything else. If I couldn't convince her I was okay, I'd likely be shipped off on the next flight to recover in a military hospital in Germany, while Fred would be stuck in Afghanistan.

I put on my best performance. I didn't stop smiling the whole time we talked. I cracked jokes. She asked about my job and my life at home. I found out she'd lived in the Washington, DC, area, and before long we were talking about the weather and Beltway traffic like we were old pals.

After about forty-five minutes, there was a pause in our conversation, and the doctor looked at me. She was smart and could probably tell what I was doing. She agreed to sign the release form with the understanding that I would go to two weeks of physical therapy in the Traumatic Brain Injury Recovery Center before returning to the field.

"You got it," I told her, grinning like a little kid.

Back at the intelligence office, I caught up with Sergio.

"Hey, man, Fred was not happy while you were

away," Sergio said. "I went over to DHL the day you got hit. I brought his favorite—roast beef—and he wouldn't eat it."

There was a 24-7 sandwich station in one of the dining halls. Before I'd left on my mission, I would go late at night and grab some lunch meat and cheese for Fred. After I left, Sergio kept up the routine for me, checking on Fred and bringing him treats. According to Sergio, Fred knew something was up.

"The DHL guys said he moped all day, too," Sergio said. "He wouldn't play soccer."

I shook my head in disbelief. I'd felt it from the very beginning. Fred and I were connected. I couldn't wait to see him.

Sergio gave me the keys to the truck and I headed toward DHL. As I got close to the compound, I glanced in the rearview mirror and saw trouble: a convoy of black vehicles was making its way up the road. It had to be a general or chief of staff getting a grand tour of Camp Leatherneck. It looked like the DHL facility was going to be part of the tour.

I pulled over and watched as the trucks drove over to the DHL compound. Once the officers went inside, I jumped out of the car and ran up to the fence. I found a hole in the netting and looked through. Where Fred had been tied up when I left, there were a few empty water bottles on the ground—makeshift chew toys—and a big hole he'd dug. But no Fred.

It looked like the general and his staff had started their tour. Tinashe emerged, clipboard in hand, and walked the group around, pointing to the whiteboard listing scheduled shipments and to a truck filled with air-conditioning units. The general pulled a handkerchief from his pocket and dabbed the sweat from his brow.

I started to panic about Fred. He was nowhere in sight, and I worried he might have run off. Or, if the DHL guys were hiding him somewhere, it was only a matter of time before he'd start to bark, giving himself away. If someone saw Fred now, his life could be in danger.

I was about to move to get a better view when I saw Peter come out of the office. Like Tinashe, he wore a DHL polo shirt tucked into khakis, and he stood upright, a bit uncomfortable. Then I saw him: Fred was trotting beside Peter at the end of a leash. His big, fluffy tail was bouncing up and down and his snout was waving in the air as always. Peter, clearly trying to act as natural as possible, led Fred to a row of crates. The two slowly walked up and down the row while Fred sniffed along the bottom of each crate. At one crate, they paused. Peter lifted the palm of his hand, then smacked the top of the crate a few times, as if patting it. Fred looked up at him. Then, sending a little poof of dust into the air, he leapt on top of it.

I couldn't believe what I was seeing: Peter was parading Fred around, pretending he was a bomb-sniffing dog. And Fred, with his confident trot and natural curiosity, looked the part.

The general seemed to have had enough. The officers shook hands with Tinashe, and they drove off.

With the general gone, I got back into my truck and drove into the DHL lot. Inside, the workers celebrated their performance by standing in a big circle and kicking a soccer ball back and forth. Fred stood in the middle, happily chasing the ball and yelping with glee.

I watched for a minute, tears brimming. The weight of responsibility I felt for Fred came rushing back to me, but it didn't feel like a burden this time. Instead, it was my mission. No matter what had happened, and what might still happen, I was resolved to get this dog home.

Eventually, Fred spotted me. He came flying over, kicking up a trail of dust and whimpering frantically with excitement. I was assaulted with love. He zipped around my ankles, popping up to lick my face, then burst away to run big laps around the compound.

"Wow, buddy!" I said. "So you're a bomb-sniffing

soccer player now, huh?"

Tinashe stepped out of the office.

"Are you okay, my friend?" he asked. Sergio must have tipped him off about my injury the last time he was here.

"Yes," I said. "I'm all right."

Then Tinashe handed me a big envelope.

"What's this?" I asked.

"Fred's freedom," he answered. "You finish getting these filled out, and he'll be out of here on the next flight."

While I was away, my sister had mailed the paperwork to Sergio. He'd delivered them to Tinashe to confirm the forms were what he needed.

I leafed through them, then sat back and took a breath. They looked good. I had Fred's ticket out. I didn't feel guilty, but the weight of what I was doing kicked up a wave of anxiety in my chest. I tapped my foot into the ground and ran my fingers through my hair.

Then I had an idea. I drove to Bastion, the British side of the base. Because they weren't part of the US military, I wasn't as worried about getting into trouble. I knew they had working dogs, so I figured they must have a vet on-site.

I found the military police and security forces office

and asked if there was a vet in the camp. He pointed me in the direction of a building nearby. When I walked in, the room looked like a normal veterinary office back home. A woman glanced up from her laptop in my direction.

I introduced myself and got to the point. "I've got this stray dog," I said. I told her about Fred and how I was trying to get him home.

"I don't need your name on anything," I said. "But just for my peace of mind, could you examine him? Make sure he isn't sick with anything?"

She looked at me, stunned. After a short delay, she said, "Can you bring him in around seven tonight? By then it should be pretty empty around here."

I picked up Fred from DHL around dusk. As we drove, Fred stuck his head out the passenger-side window and smiled. For a moment, I let myself imagine the two of us on the road back home.

The vet was waiting for us, and Fred, of course, was a charmer. He let her pick him up and put him on one of the exam tables. She checked out his ears and teeth. He even let her do a rectal exam without freaking out.

"Where did you find this little gentleman?" she wanted to know.

I just laughed. "It's a long story."

"Well, he's totally healthy," she said. "He's young!

Maybe six or seven months old. Just get him home as soon as you can and have him vaccinated once he's there."

She even wrote a note for me on paper with British army letterhead, stating Fred was cleared for travel. It wasn't an official document, but she thought it couldn't hurt.

Back at the DHL compound, I handed over all the paperwork to Tinashe: my new note, along with the forms my sister had sent.

"Well done, my friend," he said, leafing through the pages. "I can get Fred out on the next flight. But we still need a kennel. Did you get one?"

I had been so worried about paperwork that I'd forgotten about finding a kennel. I was hoping Tinashe would be able to come up with one for me.

I told him I'd figure something out. As I stepped through the door, Peter and one of his coworkers ran up to me.

"Mr. Craig! We made something for Fred."

I looked at what was in their arms and, at first, didn't realize what it was. Then it registered: they had built a homemade crate for Fred. Using chicken wire and scrap wood from around the compound, they'd constructed a kennel.

Tinashe stuck his head out the office door. "I told

them I couldn't send Fred in that thing, but they made it anyway!" he said.

I couldn't believe it. I was touched by the gesture, more than I could properly express. These guys barely knew me, and they didn't owe me anything. But they had taken time out of their busy and exhausting schedule to make a box for Fred. And they'd already done so much by keeping him safe for me.

I thanked them for their kindness. But Tinashe had told me he needed a government-approved kennel.

I promised to come up with something soon, and I headed back to the truck.

The adrenaline rush that had kept me going all day was giving way to a crash. My ears started ringing, and I felt dizzy. I gripped the steering wheel and tried to think, but I couldn't come up with a plan to find a kennel.

At that point, I realized that I hadn't eaten. Around midnight each night, the dining halls served a meal we called "mid rats." It was whatever was leftover from the day's meals: pancakes, lasagna, waffles, pasta, chicken. I collected a tray of food, sat down, and stared at it, thinking.

Could I ask the nice British vet for a kennel? I didn't want to get her in trouble. She had already been so kind. I thought about ordering a crate online or asking

Sarah to send one, but I wanted to get Fred out as soon as possible.

I was about to give up on eating when I saw a young marine sitting by himself on the other side of the hall. He looked at me and waved me over. He was a skinny, lanky kid with glasses. I didn't recognize him, but I went over.

He introduced himself as Jenkins, a private. Then he leaned across the table and whispered, "I know about Fred."

"What do you mean?" I asked, sizing him up.

"Come on, sergeant," he said. "I want to help."

I asked him what he knew.

"You need a kennel," he said.

"Can you help or are you just messing with me?" I asked.

"I can get you one," he said. He worked at the military police compound and took care of the dogs. "There are empty kennels everywhere," Jenkins said. "I can get you one. What's your room number?"

I told him. We shook hands, and he left. I didn't know how this kid knew about Fred, but I assumed some of Fred's fans must have let it slip. In the Marines, stories had a way of making their way around among the lower enlisted guys. The first three ranks—private, private first class, and lance corporal—probably make up almost 80 percent of the marine corps. Those guys do most of the tough, unglamorous work, and they watch out for one another when they can. You help your buddy because sooner or later you're going to need a hand, too. We had a nickname for it: the Lance Corporal Mafia.

When I woke up the next morning, something was blocking the door to my room. I pushed harder and found a kennel. It had a top and bottom piece made of molded plastic and a metal gate for the entrance. It was perfect. Jenkins had come through for me—and for Fred.

Sergio woke up. "Dude, this is it," I said. "Let's go!"

When Sergio and I pulled the truck into the DHL compound, I honked the horn a couple of times. Fred, who was on the end of his lead, wagged his tail. Tinashe came out of the office as Sergio and I pulled out the crate.

"You did it!" he said.

Peter and some of the DHL guys helped put the crate together with zip ties. I put a little pillow and one of my T-shirts inside—plus some food from the chow hall—and we let Fred wander in to check it out. I grabbed a black Sharpie and wrote across the top of the crate, "Sgt. Fred, USMC."

"Okay!" Tinashe said in approval once the crate was

ready to go. "Today's the day."

He walked over to the schedule board that listed the day's outgoing and incoming shipments. In the outgoing column, he wrote, "Bye to Fred, we will miss you, good boy. Love, DHL Staff."

I squatted down and held Fred's face, massaging his neck under his ears. He looked at me happily, tongue peeking out between his goofy teeth, as he panted lightly. As usual, he looked like he was smiling.

"Okay, buddy," I said. "You're going home."

I put a last piece of lunch meat in the crate and closed the gate behind Fred when he went inside. Tinashe helped me lift it onto a wide, flat pallet, then we strapped it in place. Peter drove a forklift up to the pallet and gently lifted it, placing it onto the back of the flatbed truck. Fred sat in his crate looking out, still grinning, as if this was part of a great adventure.

"Do you want to come along?" Tinashe asked. He was going to personally make sure Fred boarded the plane without any issues.

"Absolutely," I said.

Sergio and I hopped into Peter's truck, following behind Fred's truck. It was quite a view: an 18-wheeler pulling nothing behind it except a trailer with a happy little dog in a crate.

Tinashe pulled the truck onto the tarmac where a

huge white 747 was waiting. Peter and a few of the DHL guys had come along, and they jumped up on Fred's pallet for one last goodbye and a group photo.

The flight would last twenty-four hours. Fred would fly to Pakistan, then Bahrain, then Germany, and finally John F. Kennedy International Airport in New York.

Tinashe asked me to explain the special cargo to the loadmaster, a big guy with a firm handshake and long beard. He was excited about Fred and his story.

"I'll be with him through the entire journey," he said. "I miss my dog back home, so it'll be nice to have some company. He's in good hands."

A forklift loaded pallets of cargo into a large bay at the side of the plane. Fred stayed in his crate, totally relaxed. We watched until he disappeared into the airplane.

"Bye, Fred!" we shouted, and waved, a crew of dusty guys from around the world, all devoted to this funny, sweet-hearted furball.

I thought of the marines I had served with and how badly they had wanted Fred to make it home, too. I felt like I had achieved something we could all be proud of—something that meant more to me than any medal or award. I still had four months left in my deployment. The last few days in the field had nearly destroyed me, and I didn't know what lay ahead. But a deep sense of peace settled over me. I took in a long breath and let it out.

The massive jet engines began to whir, and the plane taxied onto the runway. It roared to life and sped away. At the end of the runway, the plane lifted into the sky and became smaller and smaller in the distance. I smiled and thought, *There goes my dog.*

CHAPTER 7
WHAT IF?

AFTER I WATCHED the plane carrying Fred take off and disappear into the distance, I called Sarah back in the States.

"Hey, Sis," I said. "Fred is on the way. He'll be at JFK in twenty-four hours. Can you and Dad—"

"We'll be there," she said, before I could finish the sentence.

I sent Sarah the flight details and waited to hear back from her. I was in limbo: stuck on Camp Leatherneck, going to physical therapy, working in the intelligence office, wondering about Fred. I walked around the place like a ghost—empty, going through the motions, my mind somewhere else.

Twenty-four hours felt like an eternity. Finally, the time passed, and I grabbed my satellite phone and walked outside. The stars twinkled overhead. I dialed the phone and listened to it ring. The line clicked, and I heard Sarah's voice.

"We got him," she said. "He's beautiful, Craig."

Tears of relief ran down my cheeks.

"You did it," Sarah said. "You did it!"

When I called, Sarah, my dad, and Fred were in the car driving from New York City back to Virginia. Sarah told me how, at customs, both the loadmaster and pilot had come out and introduced themselves.

"This is a great dog," the loadmaster said.

When the paperwork cleared and they finally were able to let Fred out of the kennel, he stepped out, looked around at the group of people, and then walked up to Sarah.

Someone whispered, "How did he know that's Craig's sister?"

Our conversation was only a few minutes long, but the joy we shared over the phone that night was electric. I remember the way the tone in Sarah's voice shifted before we hung up. She didn't say it outright, but I could hear it in her goodbye: she was saying, "You did this—but you're not done." I still needed to come home, too.

Neither of us knew it then, but the worst part of my deployment still lay ahead.

I was miserable at Camp Leatherneck. I completed my two weeks of physical therapy at the Traumatic Brain Injury Clinic and was cleared to go back into the field, but I needed to wait. The marines I'd worked with were still at the compound in Sangin, but their deployment was ending. In a few weeks, they'd be at Camp Leatherneck and a new company of marines would take their place. I was assigned to go in with the new company.

It felt good to hang out with Sergio and Mac, eat real food, and work out in the gym, but I wanted to be back in the dirt with my guys. I had spent too much time in the air-conditioning. Physically, I was okay. I still got dizzy if I stood up too fast or if I worked out too hard. At night, I still got headaches, but I didn't tell anyone about that.

With Operation Fred accomplished, my focus was on getting back out into the field. When I returned to my post, Justin and Ysa would still be at work as explosives experts for the team. I was eager to see them and let them know that Fred had made it home.

Right before I returned to Sangin, my sister sent me a small photo album. It was filled with pictures of Fred:

sitting in the back of the car on the way home from the airport, sopping wet and confused during his first bath, hanging out on the couch with my dad, rolling in the grass and drinking from a fountain in the backyard of my childhood home. I turned the pages over and over again, staring at the pictures. Seeing Fred back home made it feel real for the first time. I fell asleep looking at it.

After nearly a month at Camp Leatherneck, I returned to Sangin by helicopter, just like I had before. When the new marines and I reached the compound— the same one I'd been at most recently—it was as if I'd never left. I walked up to the room Justin, Ysa, and I had initially claimed, and there they were, half asleep, their mats in the same spots as before. The corner where I'd had my sleeping mat was clear, as if they had saved it for me.

I walked in and dropped my stuff, saying, "What did I miss?"

Justin and Ysa woke up and got to their feet.

"Look who's back from the one-oh-seven party," Ysa teased, referring to the 107mm rocket that had nearly killed me.

"You didn't miss much," Justin said. "Couple gun-fights and a few episodes of *Breaking Bad*."

The guys came over and hugged me. Their beards

were coming in strong and so was their body odor. I could tell that Justin—who had found the rocket in the post-blast evaluation—seemed a little surprised I was back out in the field. He asked how I was doing, but he didn't push it.

"How was the ice cream back at Leatherneck?" Ysa asked, making a reference to Forrest Gump's relaxing recovery after he got shot in the butt, in the movie *Forrest Gump*.

"Oh, it was delicious," I said. "I got Fred out, too."

I told the guys the whole story. They couldn't believe it.

"Man, you got scammed," Ysa said. "That dog's actually a Taliban sleeper agent. Now he's gonna go back and infiltrate our government. He'll hold your dad hostage."

The teasing was endless. It was what we did. Next time I went to the bathroom, Ysa said, "Here you are going to the bathroom in a bag while your dog is back home eating cheese and sleeping in your bed."

I laughed. Justin smiled and shook his head.

Over the next few days, we stayed in the compound, and the new marines became familiar with the terrain. By the fourth night, we were headed out on a patrol. The plan was the same as before: we would go into the Green Zone and take over a compound in the heart of

Taliban territory and hold it for a few days. Just as we'd done before, Justin, Ysa, and I chose to go out with the other marines.

The night started out like the others. We ducked through the doorway of our compound into the cool, dark desert, and headed toward the lush fields and canals of the Green Zone. It felt good to be back to work, and I fell right back into the routine. We slipped down the ridge, crossed the first canal, and ventured into a dense field of corn.

It was in the second field that we realized something was wrong. By the time the pointman—the leader— was about halfway across, he had sunk hip deep in rich, dark soil. The field was flooded.

We didn't have any choice but to continue. We waded into the slop. It was as thick as chocolate pudding. With each step, the mud pulled me down. We inched forward. Progress that should have taken a few minutes took nearly an hour. Finally, a few of us made it to a small hill on the opposite side. Justin passed his canteen around, along with a Clif Bar from one of his wife's care packages.

When I looked back into the field, I saw the machine gunner—a young soldier who must have been carrying his weight in gear—thrashing in the mud, quietly sinking. I left my pack with Justin and Ysa and waded over to him, taking his gun to lighten his load.

Eventually, the rest of the patrol made its way through. One of the marines lost his boot in the sucking mud. He frantically tried to recover it, but we didn't have time. It had taken well over an hour to cross the mud pit.

When we got to the next field, it was flooded, and so was the one after that. A patrol that should have taken a few hours took nearly all night. When we arrived at the compound, we were exhausted and had only an hour or two until sunup. We told the marines to rest while they could, and Justin, Ysa, and I, and a marine named Brian started filling sandbags.

The compound was small, with high walls. We strengthened a rooftop post on top of one of the rooms. We blocked an open doorway with sandbags.

By the time the sun came up, the compound was in good shape. Justin, Ysa, and I found an empty room and collapsed. We took off our boots and tried to get warm and dry. We were caked in mud from the waist down, and we had dried mud smeared across our faces, chests, and hands.

We put our sleeping mats side by side and lay close together to try to share body heat. I could tell that Justin, who was in the middle, couldn't get comfortable. I thought I heard his teeth chattering. I pulled out an extra pair of wool socks from my backpack and gave them to him. Anytime anyone back home asked me what I needed in a care package, I always asked for three things: beef jerky, instant coffee, and wool socks.

"Thanks, man," Justin said, putting them on. For a short time, we slept.

A few hours later, the attack came. When we woke up, the radio was buzzing, and marines were scrambling. The fire was rapid, constant, and accurate. The rounds sounded closer than I'd ever heard. I worried that the standoff—the space between us and the enemy—was too narrow.

Sean, the gunner who had been on the rooftop post all morning, was at the end of his two-hour shift, but he wouldn't come down. He knew it was going to get ugly. Another marine got up there and joined him.

Justin, Ysa, and I took up fighting positions against the wall. In this kind of attack, we were marines first and specialists second. I peeked through a hole in the wall and saw a narrow alley and the wall of the neighboring compound less than twenty feet away. Above us, on the roof, Sean was peeking his head above the sandbags; he had already taken out two Taliban positions, but more were popping up around us. He needed to get a visual on where the fire was coming from. The more we knew about the enemy, the more accurately we could engage them and take them out.

A loud shout came from the roof. "Corpsman!" The marine who had joined Sean on the roof was calling for the medical specialist.

My heart rattled against my chest.

"Corpsman!" They were overrun with gunfire. Sean had been shot.

I ran over to try to help. Sean had been hit right under the brim of his helmet, in his forehead. The other marine was trying to stop the bleeding from his position on the roof. We needed to get Sean down. Bullets were buzzing directly overhead, some hitting the small sandbag barrier in front of the two gunners.

The corpsman—Doc Jones—found a rope and threw it up to Sean's partner, who tied it around Sean's chest and under his arms. He lowered Sean down, over the edge of the roof. We heard Sean suck in a deep gasp of air. He was still alive.

I recognized Sean from the time we had gathered for our departure. He had asked about Fred, smiling and laughing. He had blond hair and a big, Viking-like frame. He looked young—maybe just twenty years old—but I got the feeling he was an old soul.

Doc Jones and I grabbed Sean and guided him down onto a tarp stretcher so that we could move him more easily. The lieutenant had already called for a medical evacuation over the radio.

We wrapped Sean's head with gauze and inserted an IV. His blood pressure was dropping and his breathing was shallow. I helped Doc Jones start a tracheotomy, or a hole in his throat to make it easier for him to breathe. We wiped Sean's neck with alcohol and I put my hands on his throat, right above his collarbone, holding the skin tight while Doc made a small cut and inserted a tube into the hollow of Sean's windpipe. I helped Sean breathe while Doc Jones monitored his vitals and radioed his status to the approaching medevac helicopter team. I looked at Sean's helmet, which was filled with blood, tissue, and fragments of his skull.

Sean was still breathing on his own. I'd give him two breaths, then he'd do one by himself. He was unconscious, but in case he could still hear, I talked to him.

"You're gonna be okay, man. You're a badass. Stay with us."

I felt like my hearing was heightened. Tinny sounds of the ongoing firefight surrounded me. The repeated *pop-pop-pop-pop-pop* of machine gun fire echoed overhead as marines fought from the rooftops. Doc Jones spoke rapidly into his radio. Other marines spoke to Sean: "Stay here, Sean. We need you. Don't go. Don't go." Finally, I heard the steady *thump-thump-thump* of the medevac in the distance.

As the firefight continued, two rocket-propelled grenades flew overhead, landing inside our compound. They landed with a sharp, explosive crack, sending rocks and debris erupting into the air. To my amazement, no one was hurt.

The incoming medevac was an air force team called Pedro. They came in twos: one copter was heavily armed and defended the second one, which was an airborne ambulance with a medical crew. They needed to make the dangerous landing in the middle of the firefight to try to rescue Sean.

Overhead, we saw the armed helicopter come in fast and low, spraying machine gun fire into the Taliban-occupied compounds. Close behind, the second helicopter hovered over the compound as bullets ricocheted off its belly.

Over the radio, the pilot said, "There's not enough space to land!"

He pulled the helicopter up, rotated almost 360 degrees, and zipped to the other side of the compound, toward an open field.

"We're putting it down," I heard the pilot say over the radio.

He landed in the only place he could—in the adjacent field—where the rescue team would be completely exposed.

We needed to move fast. With a count of three, Justin, Ysa, another marine, and I picked up Sean on the stretcher and sprinted toward the doorway. Sandbags blocked the passage. They needed to come down, fast. We put Sean down and yanked bag after bag away from the entrance. The longer the helicopter was on the ground, the more vulnerable it was. From the roof, the marines continued to lay down fire, providing as much cover as possible so we could get Sean to the helicopter.

We tore at the sandbags. I saw a blue hand reach through from the other side to help. It was the gloved hand of one of the rescue team. He had jumped out of the helicopter to help us clear the doorway.

With enough room cleared, we lifted the stretcher and rushed into the field, making our way toward the open door on the side of the helicopter. One of the two pilots had climbed out and was shooting toward the Taliban with his pistol. The rescue worker who had helped clear the doorway fired his rifle, covering us as we ran.

When we got to the helicopter, we lifted Sean inside. Doc Jones shouted out a final round of vitals as the pilot and rescue workers jumped in. The helicopter lifted off immediately, Sean's huge boots still hanging out the side as it climbed into the sky. Our Viking buddy was almost too big to fit inside the helicopter.

The marines on the roof screamed at us to get back inside. We could have all been killed with one spray of machine gun fire. We ran for our lives. Just before I passed through the doorway into the compound, I looked up as a round hit one of the marines on the roof in the vest. Dust flew off his body armor, but he barely flinched. He was mad. We all were.

At that point, the Taliban fighters grew bolder. They knew they'd gotten one of us, and it made them more confident. I was no longer hearing only bullets whizz by. I could hear larger weapons being fired and the voices of Taliban fighters shouting to one another close to us. They were right there. In my four months in Afghanistan, I had never seen the enemy like this.

We're gonna be overrun, I thought. Videos I'd seen of Taliban fighters overtaking coalition forces flashed in my mind. I imagined them standing over our stolen gear and defacing our stripped, mutilated bodies.

No, I thought. *That's not how my family is gonna see me.*

A 107 rocket whizzed overhead and sputtered in the distance.

"Hey—nobody take that," Ysa shouted. "That's Craig's!"

I looked at him smiling and joking, even in battle. I couldn't help but laugh.

Once again, we called for support from HIMARS,

the rockets sent from Camp Leatherneck. It was impossible to say how long we'd been fighting, but it felt like hours. With the rockets on their way, we took cover—lying on the ground, faces in the dirt, with our hands over our heads.

After the blasts, it was quiet.

No one had much to say. We didn't know if Sean was going to make it, and no news had come in over the radio. We wanted to give the other marines some space, so Justin, Ysa, and I radioed our base—the other compound—to give them an update.

I stood in the courtyard with Sean's blood on my boots and uniform, unsure what to do. I wanted to scream. Justin and Ysa came over, and we sat down to eat. The command decided our patrol would return to the other compound that night, rejoining the rest of the company. Our ammunition supply was low and our position was too vulnerable.

A few hours after sunset, we set out. After a day like that, we realized how fragile everything is. Even though we weren't safe in the compound, it still felt more secure than the unknown of the Green Zone. I wasn't looking forward to patrolling back through Taliban territory. Before we slipped between the tall, whispering cornstalks of the first field, I turned to Justin and Ysa and bumped my fist into theirs. "I love you guys," I whispered, then pushed my way into the sea of corn.

On the other side of the cornfield, we encountered another flooded field. It was worse now. The soil was so saturated, water pooled on top of the mud, reflecting glassy, glimmering streaks of moonlight. We trudged into the cold, sucking soil, sinking hip deep. Midway through the first field, one of the marines sank into it up to his chest, and Ysa and I pulled him out.

Slowly, we worked our way through one flooded field after another. It became clear this was part of the Taliban's plan. They knew we cut through fields, and they knew where we needed to go. If we were slow, stuck, and vulnerable, they could unload on us. And halfway through our retreat, they did. A *pop-pop-pop* sputtered through the mud near the patrol. Thankfully, though, it was just one guy taking inaccurate shots from far away. Our sniper went to the back of the patrol and lay in the mud, trying to get a shot at him.

To say we were miserable would be an understatement. We were mentally and physically exhausted. The mud was relentless, and the erratic shots were nerve-racking. What should have taken us a couple hours was taking all night.

With less than an hour before sunrise, we came upon a final canal. It was the one nearest to our compound, the first one we crossed when we left the desert and entered the Green Zone. We called it the Mini Helmand because of its size. It was wide and deep, one of the only canals that had a current to it instead of dead, still water. Once we got through it, our compound wasn't far off. We were almost home.

But something was wrong. As we approached the canal, I could hear it. When we'd crossed it the night before, the water had been up to our hips. Now, the current was raging, and it looked twice as deep.

When the first marine in the line attempted to cross the canal, he was almost overcome by the current. We were all exhausted, carrying heavy gear and wearing armor. We were at risk of losing our footing and getting pulled under and swept away.

A few other guys headed downstream to try to find a safer place to cross, but they didn't have any luck. Our patrol had been standing for a while in the open field. We were running out of time.

Not far away, we saw a bridge, which was more like an archway of packed mud, about a shoulder width wide.

What if we crossed there?

We discussed it. It was an obvious place to plant a bomb. After all, the Taliban knew where we were headed; they knew the muddy fields would delay us;

and they knew we'd end up here. It was risky—but so was getting caught out in the open when the sun rose. We'd be sitting ducks.

The pointman volunteered to check the bridge with a minesweeper. If there were no bombs, we'd cross at the bridge. The problem was that we never completely trusted minesweepers. They only detected metal, and plenty of bombs were made mostly of plastic. Only the switching mechanism needed to be metal, and sometimes it was the size of an aluminum foil gum wrapper. The sweeper could miss it altogether.

Fifteen or twenty minutes had passed. Occasional rounds buzzed by, slapping the swollen earth, but the gunfire would come hard and fast as soon as the sun was up.

Justin pulled Ysa aside. "I can't let that kid go up there with that sweeper," he said. "We'll be sending him to die."

Justin volunteered to go. "Let me get up there," he said. "If there's an IED, I'll find it."

In a case like this, the only way to clear the bridge was by hand in a painstaking process. Our patrol fanned out in the field, and I stood back, next to my backpack, watching from a distance. Carefully, Justin approached the bridge, sweeping the metal detector from right to left in front of him like he was looking for coins on the beach. Ysa followed about ten feet back, so he could talk with Justin while he worked. Explosives experts always worked in teams.

When he got to the foot of the bridge, Justin placed the minesweeper behind him. He crouched down and crawled forward on his hands and knees. He pulled out a knife. Then, methodically, he pressed the tip of the blade into the dirt in front of him, slowly lifting it. He moved forward, carefully digging and lifting as he searched for wires. If he lifted the knife and pulled up wires attached to a bomb, he would figure out the best way to disarm it. Or, since we wouldn't have much time, if he found a bomb, we might give up on the bridge and try to make our way through the canal.

Justin was expert at clearing explosives. He'd done it more than one hundred times on his last deployment in Iraq.

We waited in the field as Justin worked his way across the bridge.

About a quarter of the way over the bridge, Justin's knife caught something. Slowly, he lifted it, drawing two wires from the dirt. He'd found a bomb.

Cautiously, Justin got to his feet on the narrow mud bridge. He looked back at Ysa, signaling that he had found something. In the same moment, I heard a loud, deep blast, and the bridge erupted in a black cloud of dirt and mud.

I felt the blast in my body like a thud to the chest. My ears rang. Ysa was knocked backward.

I tried to convince myself that Justin was okay.

Sometimes bombs didn't completely detonate.

Sometimes they were duds.

Sometimes no one got hurt.

Sometimes everything was okay.

I heard Justin scream. I'll never forget the sound. He wasn't screaming in pain. It sounded like a cry of dis-appointment. It was as though he was apologizing—to us, to himself, to his family.

I jumped up and started running. Ysa got to Justin first, followed by Doc Jones.

At the site of the explosion, a bomb blast crushes the body. Justin's right leg was gone from his hip down. His left leg was mangled from foot to thigh.

Conscious but disoriented, he tried to say he'd found a bomb; we shouldn't take the bridge.

"Is everyone else okay?" Justin asked Ysa.

"Yes, we're okay," Ysa said. "We got you, buddy."

Justin had been thrown into the bank of a smaller canal that fed into the one we needed to cross. When I got there, Ysa and Doc Jones had already applied a tourniquet to each of Justin's legs. He was on a stretcher.

Doc Jones ran an IV and handed me the bag. Someone was on the radio. I knew we didn't have much time.

We kept talking to him. "Hang in there," we said. "Justin, you're the man. Don't worry."

Justin's breathing was labored. His blood pressure dropped. Doc placed a mouthpiece over Justin's lips with a tube attached to it. Ysa took the IV bag from my hands, and just like with Sean, I leaned over and breathed air into Justin's lungs. Every few seconds, I exhaled, and Justin's chest rose.

The guys were all there. We continued to talk to him as he began to lose consciousness. It was as though he was falling asleep.

Overhead, we heard an eerie *whoop whoop whoop* sound. Canisters of infrared illumination tumbled through the air like strange, slow fireworks. They'd been fired to provide light so that the helicopter pilots could safely land.

As the helicopter came down, we lifted Justin and ran through the mud toward its open hatch. I held the stretcher in my right hand while carrying Justin's flak vest in my left. A part of my brain was on autopilot, from training. I'd picked up his vest because I knew you were never supposed to fly without it.

We ran Justin up the ramp and laid him down among a team of trauma nurses and surgeons who got to work immediately. I dropped Justin's armor and stood there, unable to move. My face and hands were covered in blood and mud. I reached one hand out to my friend and touched his chest. Then I backed away.

When the helicopter took off, I lay facedown in the mud and screamed into the cold, wet earth until my throat hurt. My head throbbed. Nothing made sense. Part of me knew Justin was gone, but another part of me couldn't comprehend it.

Somehow, I got up. Ysa was collecting Justin's stuff at the blast site, trying to do a quick post-blast investigation. He picked up pieces of Justin's rifle that had been blown to bits, and we hooked Justin's backpack to mine so I could carry it. By now the sun was almost up. The quick response force had arrived from our compound. They put ladders into the water so we could cross the canal. We made our way back.

Ysa and I went into our little room. We started going through Justin's stuff, getting it organized. The front of Ysa's uniform was drenched in his friend's blood.

Without looking up, Ysa said, "Justin didn't make it." He'd heard it over the radio.

"I know," I said quietly. "I'm so sorry, man."

We didn't talk much that day. We all felt numb. We stayed in the room and watched *Dumb and Dumber* on my laptop between naps. At some point, Ysa called home to his wife.

Later, there was a patrol debrief meeting in the compound. The captain told the team that Justin hadn't made it. There was bad news about Sean, too. He was alive but "expectant"—meaning he was expected to pass away soon. He was being flown to Germany, where his parents could come and say goodbye.

A few nights later, we left the compound for Camp Leatherneck. For the first twenty-four hours there, I didn't do anything. Mac and Sergio and the rest of the guys gave me space. I showered and went to bed, but I couldn't sleep.

After that, I dove back into work. The detention facility was full, so I had plenty of Taliban detainees to interrogate and process. The days were long. I spent hours in the interrogation booth, followed by hours in the office doing paperwork. I kept busy. I kept moving.

The day of Justin's memorial service at Camp Leatherneck, I couldn't bring myself to go. Instead, I purposely scheduled an interrogation. I was still too angry and confused. I replayed the events of the mission over in my head, searching for mistakes. I went through all the what-ifs, over and over.

What if I'd gotten more involved in planning the patrol? I could have looked at the compound the team planned to take and realized we were too close to the enemy.

What if I'd said something differently at the canal? Maybe I could have convinced the team that the bridge wasn't an option.

What if.

What if.

What if.

Craig and Fred in Afghanistan.

Fred napping in Afghanistan.

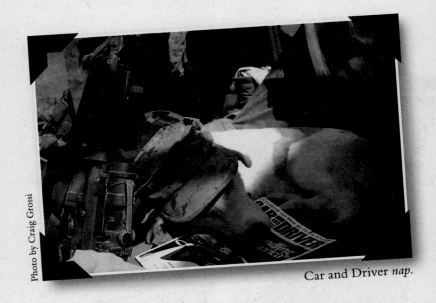

Car and Driver *nap*.

Fred napping in a bug net.

Craig holding Fred in Afghanistan.

Fred flying home.

Getting ready to hit the road.

Craig and Fred on the road.

Craig and Fred in front of the Grand Canyon.

Beach camping in Coos Bay, OR.

Fred in Maine with Ruby.

Fred and Nora.

CHAPTER 8
HOMECOMING

DURING THE FINAL DAYS of my deployment in Afghanistan, my buddy PJ and I spent a lot of time in our barracks at Camp Leatherneck talking about what we'd done. PJ and I had trained together before coming over on the same deployment. We'd been roommates, too. We thought we might serve together, but our commander separated us. He knew PJ and I made a great team, but he couldn't send two close friends into a dangerous environment. If something happened to one of us, it could make it difficult for the other to complete the mission.

Now, at the end of our deployment, PJ and I were

back together, swapping stories about what we'd seen and done in our time apart. Our deployments turned out to be relatively similar. PJ had seen some serious combat up near the dam. The Taliban wanted to regain control of the dam, so they were relentless. And since it was a known coalition base, the surrounding area was heavily laced with explosives. PJ had seen guys blow up in front of him. One moment your buddy was there; the next moment he was gone.

There aren't many words for things like that. PJ and I had seen the same things, and that was enough.

After Sean and Justin died, I went on one last, long mission. Instead of going in by helicopter, we drove out into the desert. We took a compound, one big enough that we could drive the vehicles into it. Ysa and Bobby, Justin's replacement, had cleared it before we arrived. It was turned into a patrol base. Eventually, tents, barracks, and showers would be flown in. The coalition would use it to secure the area, including the stretch of Highway 611 leading toward the dam.

On that mission, a lot of things happened in Sangin that I thought I'd never see. After a few weeks of harsh fighting, we started to see villagers moving about during the day. Kids ran around, chasing one another, playing in the sand. A local market—a little mud-walled structure by the side of the road—reopened. We started leaving the compound during the day, meeting and talking with more villagers than we had before. Ysa and I would go to the market and buy produce—cucumbers, apples, figs, and pears—almost like we were grocery shopping back home. For a while, things in Sangin were relatively peaceful. It felt like a completely different place.

Then "combat tourists" began to arrive on our base: majors, colonels, and other high-ranking leadership. They'd fly in from Camp Leatherneck and demand to go out on "presence patrols," which basically involved walking through Taliban towns in the middle of the day like a bunch of tourists. These patrols were dangerous because they didn't serve any purpose. They didn't involve talking to villagers, and the routes were loosely planned. It was as if the officers wanted to be able to say they'd patrolled in Sangin without actually spending any real time there. I didn't see the tactical benefit. To me, it was a sign that the bureaucratic war machine had caught up with us.

I was ready to go home, but I didn't feel good about getting out of there when other guys had to stay. After Justin died, Ysa and I became close, along with Bobby, who had joined us after recovering from a gunshot wound to his left bicep. He was a welcome addition to our crew of misfits. When I left, Ysa and Bobby still had another four months on their deployment. I felt like I was abandoning them, and I couldn't shake the feeling that one day I'd wake up to a call with news that something had happened to one of them.

After trading stories with PJ, I had a good night's sleep. A few days later, I'd be on a plane to Camp Pendleton in Southern California, where I'd turn in my gear and get processed out of the First Intelligence Battalion. Then I'd go home to Virginia and to Fred, who'd been waiting for almost four months for me to come home.

It was strange to be on a commercial jet in civilian clothes, but I felt good. I liked looking like a regular guy on a plane, wearing my blue Capitals cap, jeans, and a sweatshirt. On the plane, I watched movies on my iPad. I didn't feel particularly emotional. I was excited to see Fred, excited to get back and move on.

When we touched down at Reagan National Airport in Washington, DC, I walked through the terminal, and there they were: my mom, dad, stepmom, stepdad, my sister and her family, my girlfriend, and a bunch of high school buddies. They had a huge banner: WELCOME HOME CRAIG! They all wore homemade T-shirts with my face on them and waved little American flags.

I fixed a big grin on my face and walked toward

them. It wasn't a phony smile. I was glad to see them. I didn't know they were all going to be there, especially with the sign and shirts. I felt joy one minute, and then in a flash my mind went to Sean and Justin. Their families weren't going to get to have this moment. The thought sent a wave of rage and regret through my body. I felt sick.

I hadn't told anyone too much about my deployment. When I got injured, I didn't want to worry my family. I almost didn't call to tell them about my injury at all, but a couple of guys told me that sometimes there were errors in the reports sent in and the names of the Wounded in Action list were put on the Killed in Action list. I didn't want to think about what my mom and dad would feel if somehow they were falsely notified that I had been killed. So I called them both and carefully told a watered-down version of the story about the rocket explosion that almost blew me to pieces.

No one knew what I had been through. I didn't want them to worry when I was over in Afghanistan, but now that I was standing in front of everyone, it felt different. I worried that everyone would think that my injury and my time in Afghanistan had changed who I was.

I put myself on cruise control, going numb to the

noise of my emotions. I kept that smile going and took turns hugging and thanking everyone. My mom, who wore my high school ice hockey jersey, was sobbing as she pulled me in for a long, tight embrace. Then I hugged my dad, and over his shoulder caught sight of Sarah, who was crying, too. She was holding my little niece Sam, who was born just before I deployed and was now almost a year old.

My family took me to a seafood place near the airport. We were seated at a long table in the middle of the restaurant. It was crowded and noisy, and I remember looking around, thinking: Where are the exits? Where are Ysa and Bobby? I felt nervous when people were walking behind me. I watched everyone who went by, trying to listen to anything they might say.

I wasn't very hungry, but I ordered the surf and turf. Everything was drenched in butter, and I was still coming off months of bland cafeteria food and packaged meals. I ate a few bites and pushed the rest around on my plate.

No one really knew what to say. I didn't blame them. Someone eventually asked something about what it was like over there, but it was easy to deflect. "It was hot," I said with a grin.

Thankfully, there was one thing all of us were happy to talk about, and that was Fred. Sarah jumped in and started telling stories about him. On the weekends, she'd gone to my dad's house to see Fred and take him for walks. She laughed as she told me how Fred didn't understand *fetch*. He'd bring back a ball, but he'd never drop it. Instead, he'd wanted her to try to get it from him or play tug-of-war.

A few times, she talked about watching Fred sit out on the front lawn, nose up in the air, sniffing and looking into the distance. It made her cry, she said, realizing that Fred may have been wondering where I was.

"I really think he was waiting for you," she said.

My dad still lived in the house we grew up in, and my bedroom was the same it had been since childhood: same bed, same furniture, same clothes in the closet. Once, Sarah was sitting on the couch with Fred, watching TV, when she realized he'd snuck away. She called his name but didn't hear anything. After searching the house, she found him upstairs in my bedroom, on my bed, his head resting on my pillow.

When dinner finally ended, we headed back to my dad's house. On the way home, he explained how he'd turned the basement into Fred's apartment. Apparently Fred loved the carpeting down there; it offered traction for running and playing. When we arrived at the house, I raced straight to the basement. My dad had been trying to crate train Fred, so he was in a big metal crate, surrounded by pillows. As I came down the steps, the first thing I heard was his tail slapping against the metal.

"Hey, buddy!" I called to him.

His tail stopped wagging. He got a good look at my face, and I swear he did a double take. There was a moment's pause as he drew in a gasp of air, then he let out a long, slow howl, like he couldn't believe it was me.

When I opened the crate, Fred went nuts. He was all over me, jumping and nipping and flipping around. He ran between my legs, rubbing against my shins with his butt while he continued to let out excited howl-whines. I lay right down on the floor and let him jump on my chest and lick my face.

He looked like a new dog. His fur was soft and fluffy. He wore a green camouflage collar with FRED stitched on the side in big brown letters. He looked like he'd gained a little weight, too.

"Hey, buddy! You're domesticated now." I laughed, grabbing a rope toy so we could play.

I couldn't believe I was here with Fred in my child-hood home. The last time I'd seen him, he'd been in a kennel getting loaded onto a cargo jet. But something about this setting felt natural, too. Fred seemed comfortable, as if he'd always been there, as if we had always been together.

Even though it was cold and dark outside, I decided to take Fred for a walk. My family was buzzing with excitement and I just wanted a moment of quiet. I grabbed the leash, and the two of us headed out the door. We walked down a little dirt path that wound through the neighborhood. It was the same path I used to walk the neighborhood dogs on when I was a kid, longing for a dog of my own.

I was impressed by how well Fred did on the leash. He trotted alongside me, looking up every few steps as if to make sure it was really me. I smiled down at him, and we walked together in the moonlight.

In the following days, I got a full Fred report from my dad. I found it funny that my dad, who had never wanted us to have a dog as kids because he knew he'd end up doing all the work, had taken care of Fred all this time. But it seemed as if he had enjoyed it. He told me Fred had been well behaved from the start. He ate anything he was given, and he slept anywhere soft. Even though Fred had never lived in a house before, he understood potty training immediately.

Fred was smart. My dad told me that Fred quickly figured out that walks ended as soon as he went to the bathroom. Fred began holding it, forcing my dad to go on longer and longer outings before he'd finally go.

My dad found that Fred was terrified of curbside sewer drains. Something about the dark hole in the ground totally unnerved him. My dad had to avoid all drains to prevent Fred from freezing up. A few times, he had to carry Fred in his arms if they had to pass one on a walk.

Another thing Fred didn't care for was being groomed. Since his fur was long, my dad figured it would be a good idea to take Fred to a professional groomer. He dropped the dog off and returned a couple of hours later. Neither Fred nor the groomer looked very happy.

"He barks really loudly," the groomer said.

Apparently Fred had had a lot to say about his new haircut.

In general, Fred seemed happiest outside. He loved sitting out on the front lawn, taking in the smells, and rolling around in the grass. He also loved the snow. The first time he saw it, he stuck his long snout into a pile of snow and pushed it around.

My dad warned me that Fred was fascinated by wood and had chewed up some furniture in the house. He had become a bit impatient, too. One morning, my dad hurried to drink his coffee before taking Fred out for his morning walk. I guess my dad wasn't fast enough.

Instead of calmly waiting, Fred bit into the trim around the door and popped off the frame in one tug.

While I was in Afghanistan, my dad had been protective of Fred. If anything had happened to the dog before I got home, my dad wouldn't have been able to live with himself. So—aside from a few trips to the vet for vaccines and to get neutered—Fred mostly spent his time inside or on leashed walks.

Now that I was home, I couldn't wait to take Fred on adventures and to start our new life together. I quickly realized that there would be a learning curve for both of us. We were starting over, in a different city, in a different country, and we had to get to know each other again.

Even faced with summer humidity, Fred had a lot of energy. He wanted to be outside, and nothing seemed to tire him out. After I moved to an apartment with my girlfriend, Fred chewed around the base of my apartment door and along the windowsills, just like he'd done at my dad's house. Sometimes he'd start gnawing on the doorframe right in front of me, just after we came in from a long walk.

"Fred!" I'd shout, completely frustrated.

We spent a lot of time at the dog park. At first, Fred didn't understand how to play with other dogs. He had met other dogs in the past, but he hadn't really been socialized. When a pack of dogs would romp and wrestle at the park, instead of joining in, Fred would chase them, nipping at their heels and barking incessantly. He seemed to have some kind of herding instinct, but he was too aggressive. A few times one of the other dogs lashed back at Fred, and I'd have to break up a scuffle. It was never too serious, but it was scary.

I kept taking Fred to the park and watching him closely. I'd never trained a dog before, but I knew Fred needed to be socialized, and he definitely needed time to run and play. Despite the challenges with other dogs, he loved the dog park. Always a bit on the independent side, Fred was happiest off-leash when he could wander around, explore, and sniff everything at his own pace. I smiled to myself watching him bop along with his curly, fluffy tail in the air, still the confident, happy dog I had found in Afghanistan.

Every morning before I went to my new job at the Defense Intelligence Agency (DIA), I'd fill my coffee mug and we'd go to the dog park. As Fred got to know some of the other dogs, he started to relax. The next problem was actually getting him to leave when it was time to go. Even when I'd bribe him with a handful of treats, Fred didn't want to go. When it was time to leave the park, I would trick him. Fred loved to cool down in the creek that was part of the park, but separated by a gate in the fence. If I wanted his attention, I'd stand by the gate. When Fred saw me there, he'd come running, thinking he was going for a dip. As he ran to me, I'd grab him by the collar and clip on the leash so we could go home. After a couple of times, he figured out the game, and I was back to square one.

At the apartment, my girlfriend had a dog of her own, a little pug that Fred did not like. The worst moments came at mealtime. Whenever I sat at the table to eat, Fred would lie by my feet, guarding me. The pug would wander over to the table, hoping to be handed a nibble to eat, and Fred would flip out. He'd start barking and snapping, chasing the pug into the other room. This behavior caused a lot of tension between my girlfriend and me. She wanted to put the dogs in separate rooms when we ate. It was a logical solution, but I wanted Fred to learn how to behave. He was stubborn—but so was I—and I insisted on trying to teach him.

To train Fred to be less possessive, I started taking away his food while he was in the middle of a meal, or I would stick my hand in his bowl while he ate. A few times, he snapped at me. Once when he was chewing a rawhide bone—he *loved* those—I pulled it away from him, and he turned and bit me on the wrist, hard enough to draw blood.

I was mad. I grabbed him by the neck and pinned him to the floor. Fred squirmed and yowled. I held on, holding him in place, saying, "No!" We struggled like two brothers. Finally, Fred submitted. He never bit again. We both had a lot to learn about how to get along now that we were back in the United States.

CHAPTER 9
MOVING ON

THERE'S NO MANUAL ON how to come home from war. The only other person in my family with combat experience was my uncle John, who had been like a grandfather to me. He had served in World War II and fought in the Battle of the Bulge, where almost everyone in his platoon was killed. For two weeks, John was missing in action, presumed dead. During that time, he was making his way out from behind enemy lines wearing a stolen German trench coat. He escaped, survived, and made it home. According to the story, by the time Uncle John got back to the United States, he'd been shot a few times and had a nasty case of trench foot. But he recovered, settled down with my aunt Alma, had a successful career, and made a happy life for himself and his family in the Washington, DC, area.

The message was clear: you come home and you move on. That's what I planned to do, too.

Coming back to my hometown made it easy, at first. I started hanging out with my high school buddies again. I went to my ten-year high school reunion. I reunited with my girlfriend. I worked. I didn't talk much about Afghanistan because I didn't have to. I was a civilian now.

I started remaking my life, checking off all the boxes on the list of things I thought I should do. The first one was getting a job. My former commanding officer helped me get a position at the Defense Intelligence Agency. I worked as a reports officer, reviewing, editing, and releasing intelligence reports from collectors in the field.

The next box to check was getting a new car. I'd always driven beat-up trucks. This time I bought a new Toyota Tacoma. It had a shiny fresh coat of maroon paint, four doors, and the off-road package. When I drove it off the lot, it was gleamingly perfect—too perfect. It wasn't me. It came with a hefty monthly payment, too, and insurance payments like I'd never seen. I tried to convince myself that it was time to grow up.

The next box: getting serious about my relationship. Throughout my deployment, I had the same girlfriend. We had gone to different high schools, but we had mutual friends. When I got back from Afghanistan, we found an apartment and moved in together. I felt like I should propose, so I planned a vacation for us in Puerto Rico the week before I started my new job. I proposed in the hotel lobby after letting the staff know ahead of time. They stood in a circle around us and clapped when she said yes. The first thing she did was light a cigarette and text pictures of the ring to her friends.

Within a few months of being home, I had a new job, a new car, a new apartment, and a fiancée. Like Uncle John, I was moving on.

The first sign that things weren't okay came that summer when I went to Hilton Head, South Carolina, to spend the Fourth of July with my mom, stepdad, and other family. After lunch, a few of us sat out back on the patio visiting. I was fine until the kids next door launched firecrackers into the lagoon. As soon as I heard the blasts, my body responded. I grabbed my friend Nathan and pulled him to the ground to protect him. It was instinct.

In that moment, I didn't know where I was. I felt like I was back in battle.

My brother-in-law jumped up to make sure I was okay.

"I'm sorry," I said, trying to come back to my senses. My heart was racing. The *whooshing* noise the firecrackers made as they flew through the air sounded exactly like a rocket attack in Afghanistan. I got to my feet and helped Nathan up, my palms sweating.

"I don't know what happened," I said, trying to smile and brush it off. "I thought the Taliban moved in next door."

Up until that moment, I thought I was in control of my memories and experiences, but they had control over me.

I had noticed that Fred also had trouble with loud noises, like fireworks or cars backfiring. One time we were walking to a local farmers' market when a truck came barreling down the street. It felt like the sidewalk beneath us was vibrating. Fred tried to run away. I scooped him up and held him in my arms, telling him, "It's okay, buddy. You're safe."

Another time the smoke detector went off in the middle of the night. Fred jumped into bed and stayed with me, shaking, even after I had silenced the alarm. I knew how he felt because I felt that way, too.

I laughed off the incident and continued to pretend that everything was fine.

That fall, my fiancée suggested we buy a house. Her friends were moving to the suburbs and starting families. She wanted that, too, but I desperately wanted to live in the city. I was twenty-eight years old and had spent nearly all of my twenties in the marines. I tried to convince her the suburbs could wait.

She wouldn't budge. I found myself far from the city, looking at three-bedroom houses with two-car garages and big lawns. I stood in the foyer of one house, looking at the slick hardwood floors and empty rooms, and suddenly everything came crashing into focus. This wasn't me. I wasn't happy—not with the house or the truck or the job or the person I was supposed to marry. I thought that checking all the boxes would lead me to where I was supposed to go, but all I wanted to do was run.

I started unchecking the boxes.

My fiancée and I split up, and I got a studio apartment in Washington, DC. It was small, with just enough room for a couch and a bed, but it was all I needed. I stocked the freezer with microwavable burritos and used my woobie—a thin, camouflage-print military-issued blanket—as my bedspread. Every night, Fred curled up between my legs just like he had in Afghanistan.

I sold the shiny new Tacoma and bought a bike. I

rode it everywhere, including to work.

I stuck with the job, at least for a while longer. Still, coming home to Fred was the best part of my day. When I opened the door after work, he'd go nuts. Fred would scurry over to greet me, sliding across the hardwood floor and letting out joyful howls. He'd zip between my legs, jump onto the bed, jump down, and race over again. His tail wagged a mile a minute, and his whole body wiggled with glee. There was nothing better than coming home to Fred.

I'd get out of my suit and tie as quickly as I could, put on my running shoes, and we'd be out the door. We ran every day. We had a route: left out of the building, straight down to the Capitol, then a mile down the hill to the Washington Monument and the World War II Memorial, then up past the White House and back home. I loved taking in the sights of the city with Fred. It felt like we were jogging through history. This was who I was supposed to be.

When I came home from Afghanistan, people talked to me like I was about to explode. It was the same way my mom used to talk to me when I was sick. A simple "How are you doing?" could feel loaded. When I first got home from Afghanistan, I resented it. When it came to talking about Afghanistan with family and friends, I'm pretty sure I gave off an I–don't–want–to–talk–about–it vibe. I didn't want people to think something was wrong with me, and talking about it only opened the door for that possibility. So it was a long time before I ever told anyone about what happened to Justin.

After I'd been home for more than a year, Ysa called. He was still in the marines, and we talked occasionally, but I hadn't seen him since Afghanistan. Ysa and a couple of other marines were going to be in DC for the weekend. They stayed with me in my tiny studio apartment, sleeping on the floor and hanging out. It felt good to be around guys who had been to Sangin and had known Justin.

I invited my high school buddies to join us. "You need to come meet my guys from Afghanistan," I told them. I was looking forward to having my best friends all in one place.

At one point in the evening, I walked up to a conversation between Ysa and a high school friend. Ysa was telling the story of the night Justin was killed. I stiffened up. Ysa pointed to me and described how I helped perform first aid on Justin before the helicopter arrived.

I felt a cool rush of anxiety sweep through me. I thought about that experience almost every night before I fell asleep, in dream-memories—part real, part imagined—and I often relived the last moments of Justin's life by the canal. *Why didn't you stop him?* I'd ask myself, again and again.

Ysa saw that I was uncomfortable. The friends I'd known all my life didn't have a clue about that night. I'd never talked about Justin.

Ysa wore a black metal wristband engraved with Justin's name, title, and killed-in-action date and location. It was common for guys to wear wristbands like this in remembrance of friends they'd lost.

Ysa pulled off the bracelet. "This is yours, man," he said, putting it on my wrist. "I want you to have it."

A burn rose in my throat and eyes, and I couldn't choke back the tears. I broke down and a year's worth of emotion came flooding out. Ysa put his arms around me and we hugged. For ten minutes, I tried to pull it together, but I couldn't. My friends tried to comfort me, but all I could think about was Justin.

The next morning, I put a smile on my face and started talking about what we were going to have for breakfast. I brushed off what had happened the night before, but I could tell the guys were worried about me.

"You can't keep that stuff inside, man," Ysa said. "You gotta talk about it. You gotta find an outlet."

It was the first time anyone called me out on the way I was coping—or not coping. I respected the way Ysa talked to me. He wasn't babying me or treating me like I was broken. He spoke to me as one marine to another, straight and factual.

"If you're not dealing and talking, you're taking yourself out of the fight. It's not gonna end well," Ysa said.

I knew he was right.

I tried to do a better job of opening up with people. It wasn't easy, and it didn't happen all at once. Over time I learned to trust one of my coworkers, Will. He was about my age and a former marine scout sniper who had served in Iraq and Afghanistan.

At first I hesitated to share my deployment stories with Will because he had a really impressive military resume. He'd seen combat in Ramadi and Fallujah and Afghanistan. I assumed he'd seen worse in battle than I had. If he had his act together after three deployments, what right did I have to complain after one?

Will and I fell into a lunch routine where we'd go to the food court and talk about the job and what we did over the weekend. Eventually I told Will about Sangin—the nightly patrols, the firefights, the rocket that almost killed me, and, in time, about Sean and Justin. His reactions made me reconsider how much I might have been downplaying what I'd been through.

Later, I talked to my former commanding officer, and I got a similar reaction. When I told him I kept working after my brain injury and after Justin's death, he said, "Man, you stayed. You could have gone on a few missions, gotten your Combat Action Ribbon, and come home satisfied. But you stayed out there. You exposed yourself, and you got everything out of that deployment you could have. That's something to be proud of."

Talking to the guys validated me. It made me feel less alone. It also made me realize that talking made me feel better. That was a start.

Fred also helped me make sense of what had happened. I got used to strangers asking about Fred when we were out together. They wanted to know what kind of dog he was—*Is he part corgi?* was a common question—and where I'd gotten him.

I answered honestly. More often than not, when I said, "Afghanistan," people wanted to hear more. So I'd tell them a bit about the marines and our mission. Before I knew it, I was talking about war with strangers. I didn't realize it at first, but after coming home from Afghanistan, having Fred kept me from feeling isolated. I met people, and I had a chance to tell them about my experiences in a way that felt relevant and safe.

❖ ❖ ❖

It took me nearly three years to go to the Veterans Affairs hospital. I was stubborn, and I didn't want to admit there was anything wrong. I was active: I ran, mountain biked, played hockey, and went on trips with Fred. Occasionally, my ears rang, but that was the only problem I admitted.

When I first returned from Afghanistan, I had to show up at the Wounded Warrior Center because of my traumatic brain injury. The woman who examined me said, "You saw combat. You're not the same. You're different now."

I resented that. Maybe I was worried that if I went to the VA, I'd be treated as a victim and labeled with post-traumatic stress.

At work, my boss encouraged me to go and talk to someone, but I wouldn't do it. He'd heard enough of my story to want to help. As a retired marine colonel, I think he felt responsible, and he wanted what was best for me.

Eventually, I gave in. I thought a lot about a conversation I'd had with a Naval Academy neurologist at Camp Leatherneck after my injury. The doc was a brain expert; he was a pioneer of concussion testing procedures for the Naval Academy football team, and he also ran a military traumatic brain injury center.

"We know a good deal about what happens to brains

upon impact," he said. "But you were also knocked out by a blast wave, and we don't know that much yet about how that impacts the brain. The data isn't there yet. You need to keep that in mind."

The doctor compared my brain to a computer. "You know how when you drop your laptop, you can pick it up, brush it off, turn it on, and it still works, but it's not quite the same. It might operate a little slower or freeze up more than it used to. Your brain is like that. It works, but some things are different. We just don't have the resources to understand exactly *how* different."

The moral of the story was that I should keep an eye on myself and let the VA doctors keep an eye on me, too. In the years since that conversation, there were times when I shrugged off what he said, and other times when I thought more deeply about it. Between the pressure from my friends and coworkers and the words of the doctor echoing in my head, I finally went to the VA.

I knew it was going to be a hassle. It takes a full day to be processed, plus follow-up appointments. I had a head-to-toe physical, including a primary care physician who examined my body, an ophthalmologist who tested my vision, another doctor who checked my hearing, and on and on, including a psychiatrist who considered my mental health.

On the first day of appointments, I gave each doctor the rundown: I'm not physically disabled. I'm active. Look, I can even touch my toes! I'm happy. I have no thoughts of suicide. I am fine. And my physical went well: I aced my vision and hearing tests.

My final appointment of the day was with a psychiatrist. *I'll be in and out of here in fifteen minutes*, I thought.

But it wasn't that easy. The psychiatrist saw right through me within the first thirty seconds of our meeting. He was middle-aged, relaxed and soft-spoken, with kind eyes. He hadn't been in the military, but he knew what he was doing.

He asked me about the memorial bracelet I was wearing to honor Justin. Before I knew it I was telling him the whole story, even the parts I usually skipped, like my final moments with Justin on the helicopter. I got emotional, but it felt good to let it out.

"Do you think you have post-traumatic stress?" the therapist asked.

"Probably," I said.

I knew I had symptoms, such as anxiety and nightmares. I needed to be honest, both with the doctor and myself. I was ready to admit the truth: it was time for me to accept help.

CHAPTER 10
BACK TO SCHOOL

OVER TIME, I LEARNED how to trust and how to talk, but that didn't solve all my problems. I still felt stuck at work. While I'd gotten close to my coworkers, the days all felt the same, and I didn't feel like my work was making an impact. I considered going back to school. If I got my degree, I could come back to the intelligence world with more options available to me.

My commanding officer in Afghanistan had gone to Georgetown University, and he had encouraged me to apply. Georgetown had a prestigious reputation, and I didn't know if I could get in, but I liked the idea of trying. I was drawn to Georgetown because I knew it wouldn't be easy. I was nervous about going back to school, but if I was going to do it, I wanted to do it right. I figured if I was going to get my degree, I wanted to get it from the best school I could.

As a kid, I was never much of a student. I knew I was smart and I loved school, but it was hard for me to learn in a classroom. My attention span was short and my energy was high. I was diagnosed with ADHD—attention deficit hyperactivity disorder—and I started medication. It made me miserable and gave me insomnia, so I stopped taking it.

I had been in school when I learned about the marines. During my sophomore year, recruiters from all five military branches came to my high school. A representative from the navy clicked through a Power-Point and explained the benefits of joining the navy. The army and air force guys did the same thing. When the Marine Corps rep took the stage, the screen went blank.

"Maybe three or four of you have what it takes to be a marine," he said. "If you think you're one of them, come talk to me." That's all he said. It left an impression on me.

Senior year I thought about joining the marines. My dad wanted me to try community college instead. I enrolled in community college—and then the terrible attacks on the United States on September 11, 2001, happened. I wanted to serve. I enlisted in the Marine Corps after my second semester of community college in 2002. Because of the high number of enlistees after the September 11 attacks, it wasn't until March 2003 that I reported to boot camp.

At first I served as a military police officer. I thought it might lead to a career in law enforcement. I'd also heard that military police (MPs) could attend K–9 training, and I loved the idea of working with dogs every day. I ended up assigned as a guard at the Guantanamo Bay detention camp at the Guantanamo Bay US naval base in Cuba, and at a naval brig (military prison) in Charleston, South Carolina. I served for four years.

When I completed my tour, I returned home for a few months. I felt like I was drifting. I reenlisted and requested special operations. I wanted to be pushed and challenged. The recruiter didn't take me seriously; he thought I was a tough-guy wannabe. He suggested I consider Marine Corps Intelligence.

I knew military intelligence was the right fit from my first interview. I showed up in a suit. I wasn't active duty so I wasn't sure if it was okay to wear my uniform. When I arrived at the office for the interview, I knocked on the door. A short, muscled staff sergeant opened the door a crack and looked at me.

"Put these on," he said, handing me a pair of hand-cuffs.

"Why?" I said, looking down at the shiny metal restraints.

He opened the door. Two larger marines stood on either side of him. They reached through the doorway, grabbed me by the collar, and pulled me inside.

Asking "Why?" was what got me into the room. It was a test. As a marine, you're taught to do what you're told, with a "Yes, sir." But Intelligence needed marines who could think independently. I learned that anyone who put on the handcuffs got the door slammed in his face.

Growing up, I was told I was a good listener. It never crossed my mind that listening would be a job skill. In intelligence training, I learned how to question, screen, collect evidence, and interrogate. I learned how to get information from conversation. I realized being a good intelligence collector meant being able to listen and form relationships with people.

I spent six months in on-the-job training, followed by four months of classroom training. We had weekly exams, and anything less than 80 percent was failure. There were times I thought I would be dropped. I was motivated and overcame my fear of academics. I started in a class of thirty, and fifteen of us graduated. I was going to be an intelligence officer.

My experiences in the military had shaped me as a person. Now that I was applying to college, I wrote my application essay about what I'd learned from my experiences in Afghanistan. In the spring of 2013, I was accepted to Georgetown University. That fall, I started as a probationary student. If I earned a high enough grade point average my first semester, I'd be permitted to enroll full-time. Starting out part-time was a perfect way for me to test the waters.

I started by taking two classes. Within the first week, I knew I was in the right place. I had benefited from my time away from school. I was ready to dive back in.

I did well in both classes and decided to leave my job and enroll full-time. Working and going to school at the same time was tough. Now that I knew I could do the work, I wanted to devote all my energy to my education. As an adult, going to school felt different. I was excited about going to class, reading the books, writing the essays, and studying hard.

I also tried out and made the club hockey team at Georgetown. I hadn't played competitive hockey in more than ten years, but I had been playing on a veterans' team and I was still in good shape. I wasn't sure I'd get along with the kids on the team—I assumed that they'd be bratty prep-school types—but I was wrong.

They were hockey players. They accepted me with open arms. I was the starting left winger. We dominated the league, winning the championship that year. The team held the record for most titles in league history, and I was proud to be a part of the program. I was ten years older and twenty pounds heavier than most of my opponents. With my long beard and "old man strength," I developed a reputation in the league as a heavy-hitting power forward. I was alive again.

In my second semester at Georgetown, in an ethics course, we were assigned to read a soldier's reflections on his time as a prisoner of war in Vietnam and his discussion of the importance of having a positive attitude. When I read it, I couldn't help but think of Fred. When I found him in Afghanistan, covered in bugs and dirt, without any buddies or a source of food and water, he could have been aggressive or mean. But he wasn't. He was sweet. He had no reason to trust me, but he did. Even in a harsh environment, his attitude was stubbornly positive.

When we came home together, Fred was a source of light. If I was mad or upset about something, playing with him cleared my mind and made me feel calm. Simply looking at Fred was comforting. We'd been through so much together, and he understood me. We were a team.

I had been through a lot in Afghanistan. It had affected me. I was dealing with post-traumatic stress. Because of that, it seemed that people allowed me—or even expected me—to be negative and cynical. Fred not only showed me I didn't have to be that way, but he helped me be my best self just by being with me. It's not what happens to you that matters; it's how you find meaning in those experiences. If Fred could do that, then I could try to do it, too.

One of my favorite parts of school was meeting new people, especially fellow veterans. I met Josh on the first day of class. I walked into the room and spotted a tall guy in the back with a beard and a prosthetic leg. I went straight for him.

"Hey, man," I said. "Isn't it a little cold out for shorts?"

"I like feeling the cool air on my leg," he said.

I knew we'd be friends.

Josh was twenty-nine years old, a few years younger than me, and from Minnesota. He had an easy-going personality but he liked to push his personal limits. Before his injury, he'd been in peak physical condition. He was tall—about six foot one—with a lean, athletic build. He could bench two hundred pounds and hike ten miles with an eighty-pound backpack, no problem.

He had to relearn how to do everything with one leg.

One night we swapped our stories from *over there*. Josh had been an infantryman in the army for about four years when he deployed to southern Afghanistan. He described the beginning of his deployment as pretty routine. He was in a mounted vehicle unit, which meant the team could travel a lot farther than traditional infantry companies did on foot. The vehicles—called Strykers—looked like tanks but with huge wheels instead of treads. Each one typically carried eleven guys. On their initial patrols, they engaged in some back-and-forth fighting with the Taliban.

Josh had been in the country only about three months when his vehicle hit a roadside bomb that took his leg. It was a routine patrol on a clear day in September 2009. Josh was in the first vehicle in the convoy, on the machine gun, sitting half in and half out of the vehicle. When the Stryker hit the pressure plate, the IED exploded directly under it. The blast took Josh's right leg and the lives of three soldiers inside.

After several months and several surgeries, Josh was up and walking. He made steady progress, but follow-up surgeries made it hard for him to get on with life. How could he keep a job if, as soon as he got one, he'd have to request several months off for surgery?

Still, Josh stayed positive. Understandably, he was

more comfortable talking about what came after the accident than the accident itself. He appreciated the health care he received, and he was always happy to show me—or anyone who asked—his leg and how it worked. Josh was grateful to be alive, and he wanted to move forward.

I talked about making a cross-country trip in the summer, and Josh offered to be copilot. "You'll get twice as far for half the cost," he said. Our road trip had a simple plan: drive west until we met the ocean, then north until we hit Seattle, then east until we reached home again.

It was an easy decision to bring Josh along. We packed my truck with camping gear—tents, sleeping mats, charcoal, and knives, as well as a football, a Frisbee, and two mountain bikes. Josh had a new prosthetic leg, complete with a robotic knee, and he hadn't had the chance to put it to the test. I was in school full-time, but I had the summer of 2015 off. I wanted to make the trip before graduating and getting back to the grind. In other words, this was our chance, and we were ready to seize it.

CHAPTER 11
ON THE ROAD

JOSH AND I set out for our journey in my royal blue 1988 Toyota Land Cruiser, headed for the green-blue Smoky Mountains in North Carolina. We sang along with Johnny Cash on the radio, and Fred popped his head between us from the back seat. "You like the music, buddy?" I asked. Fred let out a long, dramatic yawn, complete with a little whine, then curled up again on his nest of blankets and pillows. He had the best seat in the house.

We wanted the chance to see something new, to encounter the unexpected, to have each day start with that anticipation of the unknown. At that point, it'd been four years since I left the Marine Corps. I'd be lying if I didn't admit that I was in search of a taste of the life I led in Afghanistan by coming on this trip. That might sound crazy, but it's real. Every vet I know at one point or another longs for the day-to-day urgency and uncertainty of life in a combat zone. When you don't know what the day's going to bring, when your only goal is to keep yourself and your buddies alive, everything is stunningly simple. Once you get a taste of that, a lot of things you do at home just don't feel the same.

We spotted a turnoff and pulled over. "Stay here," I told Fred.

Josh and I went down a steep staircase to a river. We watched the white water wash over rocks and boulders, creating a sound like churning thunder. We stood on the edge for a few minutes and cooled down in the mist. When we turned back, I saw Fred waiting in the path. He must have jumped out of the car window. He had never left the truck before. I worried that he could have been lost. But I knew he just wanted to be with us. We were a pack now.

"C'mon, buddy," I said softly. I pulled Fred close and kissed him on the forehead. "I'm not gonna leave you."

I opened the car door and Fred leapt up onto his seat, then Josh and I climbed in. We pulled onto the winding road and made our way. Our journey was just beginning.

❧ ❧ ❧

Back in the truck, Josh and I wound through the mountains, edging closer to our first overnight stop: Chattanooga, Tennessee. It was dusk when we arrived and met up with my childhood friend Mike and a group of his friends. I hadn't seen Mike in years, but we picked up right where we left off.

We ate dinner at a fried chicken place near Mike's house. After eating we walked down to an outdoor bar so that Fred could sit with us. Mike and Josh walked ahead, getting to know each other while Fred and I followed. I smiled at seeing one of my childhood friends walking side by side with one of my newest buddies.

We were hanging out when one of Mike's friends asked me, "So, what kind of dog is Fred?"

Fred didn't look like other dogs, and he was charismatic. People were drawn to him. Sometimes he'd make eye contact with someone on the sidewalk, and next thing I knew, the person would say, "Oh my gosh, where did you get this dog?"

I told the truth. "I found him in Afghanistan a few years ago," I said. "He was way too cool to leave behind."

Mike's friend looked up at me. Between the memorial bracelets we wore, Josh's prosthetic, and my cutoff camouflage shorts, we weren't fooling anyone. It was clear that Josh and I were vets.

"Fred has a great story," Mike said. "He followed you around on patrols, right, man?"

I told the guys where I found Fred, describing Sangin and our mission there. I told them how amazed we'd been at Fred's friendly behavior in the compound. We had landed in Fred's territory, and he welcomed us.

As I told his story, Fred napped on the sofa next to me.

I liked talking about Afghanistan in a way that civilians didn't expect. Every vet battles assumptions, and it can be frustrating, especially when someone wants to know if you're "okay." I don't mind answering sincere questions, but it's never simple. Sometimes someone asks, "What's it like over there?" like they're asking about the weather. It's hard to fit the answer—a big, complicated, messy thing—neatly and casually into a few sentences. I try to keep my response light, but sometimes I do get a chance to elaborate. That's what Fred's story allowed me to do: to say more, to go into detail.

While Josh and I were talking with Mike and his friends, a couple of clean-cut guys wandered over and stood near us. They were big guys, tall and muscular. Their straight backs, clean shaves, and cropped haircuts were a dead giveaway: they were marines.

They introduced themselves. They were, in fact,

infantry marines who had done tours in Iraq and Afghanistan. They had recently separated from the marines and moved back to Tennessee to attend school.

"Did you lose your leg in combat, sir?" one of them asked Josh.

"Yup," Josh said. "I put it down in the middle of a firefight and forgot where I left it."

Our new friends grinned. Josh's sense of humor about his injury always put people at ease. "And don't call me sir," he added. "I was an enlisted guy just like you."

We talked about where we'd served and what our roles were over there, as well as being home and going to college as vets. Eventually the conversation turned to Fred.

"I can't believe you got Fred outta there, man. It's good to hear someone was able to pull it off," one of the marines said. "When we were over there, we had Maisy."

"She was the best," the other marine said. They explained that their unit had come across Maisy on one of their deployments in Afghanistan. Just like Fred, she'd become a companion to the marines, even sleeping with them at night when it got cold, curled up on their mats. Maisy was bigger than Fred, with long legs and a furry, speckled coat.

The two marines had worked in route security, patrolling the established routes that were used to move supplies from base to base. It was a dangerous job because they were vulnerable to Taliban attacks.

After long days on the road, Maisy would greet them. She also followed them from base to base when they moved. "She always found us, no matter how far we moved or how hot it got," one of them said.

From their tone of voice, I knew what was coming.

When the unit reached a permanent base, Maisy followed them. The marines made a bed for her out of old pillows and blankets. The unit had gotten so attached to her that they'd begun the formal process of requesting permission to have her sponsored by a US nonprofit that could help get her home.

One day while on patrol, the guys were ambushed. One of their teammates was shot and killed, probably by a sniper's bullet. It was a devastating day.

When they got back to their base, they looked for Maisy, but her bed was empty. There had been a few other stray dogs on the base, but they were gone, too. While the guys were out patrolling, the command had ordered the dogs put to death.

The two marines wiped the corners of their eyes. I looked over at Fred, still stretched out on the couch. When we were in Afghanistan, my biggest fear was that the same thing would happen to Fred.

It wasn't the first time I'd heard a story like Maisy's. In a combat zone, the leadership considered dogs a threat to good order and discipline. There were fears about diseases and distractions that could compromise the focus of a unit. What if the unit was put in a situation where one of the guys risked his life—or the life of a fellow marine—to protect the dog?

"I'm so sorry, man," I said. I knew they would understand that I wasn't just talking about the dog, but also about the teammate they lost—and all our lost friends.

Back in Afghanistan, Fred had been my companion and comfort, but now that I was home, he played another role, too. In everyday conversation, it seemed impossible to swap stories with other veterans about the buddies we'd lost. How do you even start a conversation like that? Fred gave us a place to start, a way to talk about some of the things we didn't want to say but probably needed to. He gave us a way to talk about war.

On Monday morning, Josh and I loaded up the Land Cruiser and headed for Mississippi, hoping to camp and catch some authentic blues music. We planned to stop in Clarksdale, where we wanted to hear the blues with the locals.

We rolled into town just before dinner and checked into a cheap motel. Josh and I headed out to look for some good music. We followed the sound of a howling guitar to a run-down place. Inside, metal chairs surrounded a few shabby tables, and worn posters and signs covered the walls. The ceiling sagged so low I could touch it. In the middle of the room, an old guy in a blue suit and tie leaned back in a wobbly chair, plucking away at the guitar. He must have been in his eighties, but his fingers moved like lightning over the strings. Behind him, a drummer played along.

We bought a couple of drinks and the owner, Red, welcomed us. When he saw Josh's prosthetic, he said, "You're wearing shorts?"

Josh smiled. "Yeah, man!" he said. "It's hot down here."

Red said his cousin had lost his leg to an infection a few years ago and had been too embarrassed to wear anything but long pants ever since.

"If I got him down here, would you talk to him?" Red asked.

"Of course," Josh said.

A few minutes later, Red's cousin showed up. He was taller and younger than Red, with dreadlocks that fell below his shoulders. He walked with a cane.

Red pointed to Josh and said, "See, shorts!"

He introduced himself as Riley. "How'd you lose yours?" he asked.

"My vehicle hit a roadside bomb in Afghanistan a few years ago," Josh said. "Let's see what you've got going on. Red says you're a fellow member of the peg leg club."

Riley rolled up the leg of his jeans. He had his knee, but below it was a carbon fiber tube attached to a shock absorber ankle and a foot that went into his black sneakers. Airbrushed onto the shin of the prosthetic was the blue and silver star of a Dallas Cowboys logo.

"I see why you wear pants all the time with that thing painted on your leg," Josh teased. Red and Riley both laughed.

Josh offered some advice on prosthetic care. He removed his leg to show Riley the sock he used to prevent irritation. Josh and Riley understood each other.

"I never would have thought I could wear shorts," Riley said.

"It's one hundred degrees here!" Josh said. "There's nothing to be ashamed of."

The four of us stayed and talked well past closing.

Josh's prosthetic offered another way to talk about war. Anywhere he went, he'd get questions about his leg. Even if Josh didn't talk about Afghanistan with every person who asked, he could if he wanted to. That's what Fred did for me, too. If I hadn't had him, no one would have guessed that I was a combat veteran, and I wouldn't have had the chance to connect with people in quite the same way.

When I came home, one of my biggest challenges was feeling alone, isolated, without direction. Working and going to school were important, but they couldn't compare to the closeness and sense of purpose that came with serving together in war. Where do you go from there? Figuring that out was one of the reasons Josh and I were on the road. The more people Josh and I talked to, the less isolated we felt. The conversations and connections felt good. One of the symptoms of isolation is feeling that people don't care and aren't interested in your experiences or your pain, but we were starting to see that that just wasn't true.

We followed the Mississippi River south to the Kisatchie National Forest, a 900-square-mile park in central Louisiana full of bayous, bogs, prairies, and woods. We chose the destination because neither of us had ever heard of it, and no one had recommended it, either.

Inside the park, we spotted a stack of maps in a plastic dispenser hung from a lonely wooden sign. "Wow, this place is *huge*," Josh said, studying the network of forest and trails.

We turned off on a trail marked for four-wheel vehicles. This was exactly the sort of road-less-traveled we were after. We bounced over the bumpy trail, rocking back and forth as we drove over shallow ditches and bumps. We found a campsite and set out to collect logs and kindling for a fire. As I picked up sticks and twigs, I saw a small stack of rocks in my path.

Don't step there! I thought, a lightning bolt of anxiety flashing through my mind. It was nothing—a little pile of stones, one balanced on top of the other, a little sculpture that served no purpose other than to mark a trail. In Afghanistan, the Taliban often stacked rocks like that to signal the location of the explosives to one another and to the villagers. I had been trained to spot these formations and to be cautious of them. The Taliban used other things to mark bombs: a piece of trash, a wrapper, a soda can—anything shiny or out of place that we might grab or kick.

The feeling of living in a minefield didn't leave me when I got home. After I came back from my deployment, I avoided going near trash or rocks as I walked down the sidewalk or through a park. On the trail in Kisatchie, a jolt of adrenaline washed through me like a wave, then passed. I reminded myself that I was home now; the rocks were just rocks. I looked up and there was Fred, bounding through the brush. I was safe.

Our adventure continued as we drove across Texas and New Mexico, driving toward the South Rim of the

Grand Canyon. Our plans changed when we arrived at the park and learned that all the campsites had been booked for weeks. We didn't want to struggle with the crowds and tourists. We decided we would go in and snap a few photos first thing in the morning, then be on our way.

Nothing could have prepared me for the view. The canyon looked unreal, like a painting. Layers of brown, red, orange, and black stretched out in layers against the bright, cloudless sky. The depth and expanse was dizzying—incomprehensible. Josh, Fred, and I stood in silence, awed by the beauty.

We took a few pictures, including some of Josh standing triumphantly with his hands on his hips and a few with him holding his leg above his head. When it was my turn, I scooped Fred up and propped him across my shoulders. We both smiled for the camera, the mighty Colorado River and massive canyon at our backs.

Taking one last look at the view, I felt insignificant. The canyons carved into the rock represented the passage of time. I knew my story was just one. Yet, standing there with my dog and my friend—two beings I never would have met had my life gone another way—I was in awe of the profound unlikelihood and beauty of it all.

CHAPTER 12
WITH A LITTLE HELP FROM OUR FRIENDS

FOR TWO GUYS, a dog, and an almost thirty-year-old truck with no air-conditioning, driving from the Grand Canyon to Los Angeles—about eight hours through the Mojave Desert—is a challenge. Every so often, wind gusted through the car, leaving behind a fine coating of sand on the dashboard and our skin, even working its way between our teeth. We loved it.

"Fred probably thinks we're taking him back to Afghanistan," Josh said.

I looked in the rearview mirror and saw Fred, still asleep in the back, unbothered by the desert air whipping through his white fur.

Farther west, signs of civilization appeared on the landscape: billboards, strip malls, and parking lots. As we approached Los Angeles, we came to a crawl on the freeway. We inched toward our exit. We planned to spend the night with Josh's friend Kyle. Josh and Kyle had deployed together but hadn't seen each other since Afghanistan. Kyle had been a sniper. During a gunfight with the Taliban, he had been shot in the arm.

Kyle met us outside his apartment building, wearing a tank top, cutoff camouflage shorts, and flip-flops. His blond hair fell to his shoulders, though some of it was stuffed in a bun on top of his head. He looked as if he had come from a day of surfing or from a music festival.

With a big smile on his face, Kyle gave Josh a warm hug and a pat on the back. Turning to me, Kyle said, "You must be Craig—and *this* must be Fred! I've heard a lot about this little guy. Welcome to LA, Freddy!" He bent down to pet Fred, and I smiled at Kyle's Southern California accent.

We went upstairs to Kyle's fourth-floor unit, where the low ceilings made the place feel dark. Dirty dishes filled the sink and covered the counters; shoes and old magazines littered the living room floor. Jimi Hendrix and Bob Dylan posters hung on the walls, next to an American flag. The apartment reminded me of a college dorm room. I wanted to open the shades and let the air and light in.

Fred jumped onto the couch and made himself at home while Josh and I took turns showering off the desert dirt. When I came out, Kyle had put on the nineties action flick *Point Break*.

"I love this movie," I said, sitting down next to him. It had been in regular rotation for movie night back at Camp Leatherneck.

In the morning, we thanked Kyle and headed off. Driving away from his apartment, Josh sighed. He started to apologize.

"It's fine, man," I said. I understood how he felt. Josh knew Kyle as a sniper in the army, back when Kyle had a clean shave, wore a uniform, and performed one of the most physically and emotionally demanding jobs in the world. Now, it seemed like he might not be doing so well.

"I'm not sure what to think," Josh said.

"Yeah, it's tricky, man," I said. "It looked like he was paying the bills. He's in school. He's probably happy, you know?" Josh hadn't known Kyle before the army; maybe this was how he'd always been.

As veterans, we didn't spend time talking about post-traumatic stress, asking personal questions, exchanging notes about how we were doing.

Everybody's experience is different. Post-traumatic stress looks different in different people. Some vets experience painful, debilitating post-traumatic stress. Others can hide it. And some may not feel it at all. It's a mistake to assume anything; that only feeds the idea that all combat veterans are "broken."

We made our way to Venice Beach, a neighborhood in Los Angeles, to visit my buddy Casey. The beachside walk was a circus. Josh, Casey, Fred, and I took in the sights: masked unicyclists, tattooed jugglers, oversized bodybuilders, and face-painted performers. When we stopped to watch a juggler, Fred's eyes followed the balls, waiting for one to drop. It was a beautiful sunny day. Palm trees rose up overhead, the mountains looked down on us from the distance, and the Pacific Ocean sparkled. *So this is what all those California songs are about,* I thought.

Casey and I met during intelligence training. Our paths crossed again briefly at Camp Leatherneck, but we hadn't seen each other since then. He was a friend for life; it was easy to pick back up.

Off the boardwalk, we stopped by a skate park. A DJ played hip-hop while an announcer called out names of skaters when it was their turn to show off and push the limits of gravity and physics. Fred sat quietly and enjoyed the entertainment, even though back home he usually tried to chase skateboarders. One of the skaters took a spill in front of us, and Fred let out a high-pitched yowl—*OOOH!*—as if to say, "*Ouch!*" His reaction drew some laughs from the otherwise tough-looking crowd.

We spent the week at Casey's place, enjoying some downtime in the air-conditioning. In the mornings, Fred and I would walk, then go to the rooftop deck to enjoy the cool morning ocean breeze.

I got in touch with someone else I hadn't seen since Afghanistan: Top. He lived in Oceanside, just a couple hours south, and invited us to come down. Top hadn't seen Fred since the day he helped me smuggle him onto the helicopter in Afghanistan. I couldn't wait to reunite them.

Top lived just outside of Camp Pendleton, the base where I'd been stationed before and after my deployment. Pulling into the neighborhood, we drove by big suburban houses with United States Marine Corps flags on front porches and eagle, globe, and anchor Marine Corps emblem stickers in the car windows. Top's house was no exception.

When we arrived, Top walked through the open garage door. He looked the same—broad shoulders, huge frame, slicked-back hair, huge smile. He wore a

Harley T-shirt, shorts, and flip-flops.

"Hey, boys!" he said. "Where's that stubby-legged guy that used to leave his chewed-up rope on my sleeping bag?"

Fred pulled frantically at his leash. I let go and he ran right up to Top, howling with joy. His body wiggled and waved from snout to tail.

Top squatted and Fred ran into his arms, gleefully shivering and spinning. Top scooped him up and cradled him like a baby. The dog licked his face and nuzzled his salt-and-pepper hair.

None of us expected Fred to react the way he did. It had been five years, and the last time he'd seen Top was half a world away. Time and distance didn't matter. To Fred, it seemed that no time had passed.

Top held Fred in the crook of his left arm as he walked over to Josh and me. He shook Josh's hand and introduced himself, then pulled me in for a long hug.

"Good to see you, brother," he said before releasing me. "Thank you for coming.

"And it's really good to see you, you little weirdo," he said, looking Fred in the face. They were both smiling so big their eyes disappeared.

Inside, Top's wife, Tara, greeted us. "We're so glad you're here," she said. "This guy's been pacing around all day waiting for you to arrive."

"I know who he's really excited about seeing," I said. Fred hadn't left Top's side.

Tara knelt down and gave Fred a big kiss on his head. "Thanks for looking after my man while he was in your country. I'm so glad you made it back safe and sound."

From the glass door leading to the backyard, Top's three dogs—two German shepherd mixes and one smaller one—stared at us, pressing their snouts to the glass. Top was a dog person.

We went out back and let the dogs introduce themselves as only dogs can. After a minute or so, they seemed to reach an understanding. Fred instantly picked out Top's biggest dog, Sugar Bear, as his new best buddy. They began chasing each other, spinning around and trying to nip one another's legs.

With the dogs romping around, I turned to Top and said something about looking forward to dinner. He looked me in the eye and said, "It's Mark. I don't go by Top anymore."

Every rank in the Marine Corps has a nickname and the master sergeant is Top, so in Afghanistan that was all we ever called him. Some retired guys still liked to be called by their rank after getting out. Top had spent more than twenty years in the marines—a rare and remarkable achievement—but he had clearly given the issue serious thought. If he wanted to be called Mark, I was sure he had his reasons.

It was a perfect Southern California day: mild with a bright blue sky overhead. When Fred got tired, he sat on Mark's foot, turning his head to look up at him. I pictured Mark and Fred alone in the command center in Sangin, sitting together on the nights the rest of us went on patrol.

Mark leaned down and petted Fred around his ears. "One time over there, I caught this little guy stealing jerky from my pack. He sniffed it out somehow. He had his whole face buried in my bag up to his eyeballs before I caught him," Mark said, smiling. "I was too impressed to be mad at him. Gave him half the bag."

"Well, you were pretty much his personal chef," I said, remembering how I caught Mark slipping Fred little bites of food around the compound. Sometimes, after we got a drop-off of fresh meals, the guys would tear open several dinners and not finish them all. Mark hated the waste. He would gather the leftovers and mix food for Fred. Once he took half a meat loaf patty and mashed it up with pasta shells in white sauce. Fred, of course, loved it.

One by one, Mark's three daughters came home from school. They were in high school, with the oldest getting ready to go to college. Like Tara, they were polite and well-spoken, pulling up chairs and talking with us. When everyone was home, we went inside and sat around the dining room table for a proper dinner. I couldn't remember the last time I'd shared a family meal. I was grateful, and the food was delicious.

Over dinner, I told the girls what an honor it was to work with their dad in Afghanistan. He didn't need to yell to get people to follow him. I followed him because I wanted to be like him; I wanted to be around him, and I didn't want to let him down. I also thanked him for keeping us safe in Afghanistan. It was his leadership and the decisions he made for the company that kept us out of harm's way.

"We were really lucky," Mark said modestly.

After our deployment, Mark retired. I could only imagine the impact he'd made on the lives of so many other marines like me.

Driving back to Los Angeles that night, I thought about Kyle and Mark. It was easy to assume that Mark's post-Afghanistan life was going more smoothly than Kyle's. But I also knew we'd only gotten a peek into their lives, and there was no way to tell how either of our buddies was making sense of their own combat experiences. For Mark, did having a family and a house help, or had it made it even harder to readjust? Did Kyle's relaxed lifestyle with fewer responsibilities help him ease back to post-army life, or did he feel isolated?

I didn't know the answers. Every soldier's reaction to combat is different. I struggled to feel anything at all when I came home. The bar for what excited and moved me had been set impossibly high from my time in Afghanistan. I had seen death up close, and it gave me a sense of how fragile life was.

My experience also made me somewhat indifferent to people's feelings. "It could be worse" became a common phrase of mine. I didn't explain my feelings. I carried on with my life, connecting with friends from home. Inside, a part of me wanted to scream for help, but I didn't. I didn't think I had the right to. I had too much to be thankful for—I made it home, I had all my body parts, I had a great dog and a fun group of friends.

I was proud. When I got home, I didn't want to be told I was "sick" with something like post-traumatic stress. I didn't want to feel like a victim or be treated like one. I knew post-traumatic stress had nothing to do with being strong or weak or with having enough willpower or not, but it still took me a while to listen to that voice inside me and find my way.

CHAPTER 13
INTO THE WILD

AFTER TEN DAYS in Los Angeles, Josh, Fred, and I headed north, up the coast. As the city faded behind us, we drove along the Pacific Coast Highway, awed by the view. Josh and I had researched a hike in the Los Padres National Forest that would take us deep into the wilderness. We planned to spend two nights in the woods, exploring hidden hot springs and creeks. To get to the hot springs, we had to cover extremely challenging terrain under full pack weight. Josh was up for the adventure. I hoped his prosthetic would be, too. It was our first overnight hike of the trip—something we were both looking forward to.

The trail into the forest started with a steep climb. We were out of breath quickly. Overhead, towering redwoods reached for the sky, blocking most of the sun but also preventing the ocean breeze from reaching us. The trail was hot. Without saying much, we pressed on, Fred panting at my heels.

After an hour or so, we reached the top. Leaning against a boulder, we rested the weight of our packs while Fred found a cool spot under some bushes. From the ridgeline we saw a vast piney wilderness to our east and the glittering Pacific Ocean to our west. The cool ocean air reached us again, rushing up the mountainside and washing over us. Looking down, we could see the long, zigzagging trail we'd just traveled.

The next few miles were flat. Josh's prosthetic leg had survived what we hoped had been the most challenging part of our hike.

Back in the parking lot, before we began our climb, a few hikers coming off the trail told us the hot springs were crowded and campsites were hard to come by. They tipped us off to a different spot—a quiet, tucked-away area with a beautiful stream running through it—and we marked it on our map.

We decided the freshwater creek sounded more appealing than battling for space at the hot springs. A trail sign pointed toward a well-worn path to the hot springs. To the left we saw the unmarked trail our friends had mentioned. Josh eyed the trail apprehensively.

"Downhill will be tough for me right now, man," he said. His prosthetic knee contained oil that became thin and less effective when hot. After a few hours of intense hiking in the heat, Josh noticed his knee giving out every so often. It's one thing to trip and fall on a trail, but it's more dangerous to fall while carrying a heavy pack and with a prosthetic leg.

"My knee is red hot," Josh said, touching the metal on his knee.

"We can go as slow as we need to," I said. "We have plenty of light left. I won't leave you behind."

A young couple came bounding down the trail from the hot springs. "Oh, hey! You guys heading to the hot springs?" the guy asked.

"Oh, yeah," I said. "Lots of people out there?"

"It's a popular spot for sure," he said. "You guys will have fun."

Josh and I shook our heads. "Let's go, man," Josh said. "I'll slide down the hill if I have to." We hadn't come all this way to share an overcrowded campsite with a bunch of noisy vacationers.

"That's my boy!" I said. I picked up Fred's leash, and the three of us walked into the woods, heading down the unmarked trail.

The trail led down the other side of the ridge through thick brush. We lost the path, but I tried to forge the easiest path for us, avoiding fallen trees and sharp drops. Josh was too busy watching his footing and bracing himself for a fall to realize we weren't on a trail anymore. Fred pranced along right at my heel, not caring where we were going as long as we all stayed together.

My thighs burned and my toes hurt from crashing into the front of my boots with every step. When I gained too much ground, I stopped for a minute to wait for Josh. He wasn't talking much. I could only imagine the mental and physical challenge he was facing with each step. As the brush got thicker and the terrain got steeper, I worried that we'd made the wrong decision.

Then I heard a low and steady babble below us. The hushed gurgles were the sounds of a stream.

"You hear that, buddy?" I asked. Josh stopped and looked up, the sweat dripping off his nose.

"Sounds like heaven," he said with a big grin.

After a few more yards, we burst into a clearing and came to a creek about twenty yards across, with a small waterfall cascading over rocks and the trunk of a massive fallen tree. It was beautiful. We crossed the shallow water in front of us and headed up the other bank. Someone had camped there, leaving behind a rock fire ring and a large log, but we walked past it in hope of finding a spot we could make our own. A few minutes later, we found a bend in the creek where the force of the water had created a small gravelly beach. A collection of boulders in the middle of the stream created a deep pool of clear mountain water, perfect for wading.

"I officially declare this Man Camp," I said, letting my pack slide off my back and hit the ground with a thud. I sat on a log and untied my boots.

Josh sat on a boulder and removed his prosthetic to give his leg some air. The nub that remained on his right leg was swollen and red. "You go check it out," he said. "I'm right behind you."

I walked onto the rocky beach in my swim trunks, Fred beside me. I stepped from rock to rock across the stream, and Fred followed, carefully balancing on the stones. I climbed onto a boulder and looked down into the deep, clear water, where a few large fish were swimming. I hopped off the rock and plunged into the cool water. The shock of the cold woke my senses. I came to the surface and sucked in the fresh air, beaming.

Fred, part panicked and part excited, waded into the water and paddled toward me, his snout in the air.

"Hey, buddy!" I said. Fred loved being in the water, but he preferred being able to touch the bottom. We floated over to the bank so he could get his footing.

"Looks cold!" Josh said from his spot on the bank. "I'm gonna jump over there." He pointed upstream to where a massive fallen tree lay across the creek. It was easier for him to jump than to wade in from the bank, hopping on one leg.

Josh left his leg on shore and scooted out on the log until he was over the pool of water. Fred went out ahead of Josh, scurrying onto the trunk, looking from Josh to me and whimpering.

"It's okay, pal," I said. "It's just a little water."

Josh looked down. He was about fourteen feet over the water, and with the boulders along the sides of the pool, he had to aim carefully. Josh lifted himself with his arms and popped off the log. He let out a "Yip!" just before hitting the water. He stayed under for a moment, then he surfaced, taking in a big breath and then smiling from ear to ear.

We spent the rest of the day swimming in the creek. As the sun set, we lit a fire at our campsite to keep the bugs away. We dined on freeze-dried camp food: chicken and rice for me, chili mac for Josh. It reminded me of military food, but with more flavor. Fred gobbled down his dinner and curled up by the fire. He had worked up an appetite playing lifeguard all day.

We were exhausted and went to bed early. The clear sky showed no signs of rain so we slept with our tents uncovered. I crawled into my tent, and Fred followed. He assumed his position curled up between my legs, his head resting on my thigh.

The next morning, Josh and I woke up rested but sore. Over a breakfast of oatmeal, dried fruit, and instant coffee, we decided to spend the day enjoying our campsite by the creek. We each found a spot along the water and read. Fred hopped around the rocks and found a perfect chewing stick. He dragged it to a big, flat boulder and gnawed away in the sun. When the day got hot, I jumped into the creek to cool off, and spent the rest of the afternoon in and out of the water. It was perfect, relaxing and recuperating.

The next morning, we packed up. I knew we were pushing the limits with Josh's leg. The leg had a battery-powered knee that acted like a shock absorber. And the battery had to be charged every three days in normal day-to-day conditions. Our strenuous hike, plus another day walking over rocks, hardly constituted "normal."

Instead of trying to find the trail, we headed straight up to the ridge. It was rockier than I remembered. I felt nervous about Josh's leg, knowing he was working twice as hard as I was to scramble up the hill.

We pushed through the thick brush and gradually made our way up the steep mountainside. As we got higher, the canopy thinned, and we began to feel the fresh ocean air. After about a mile, our trailblazing paid off, and we discovered the main path and emerged like two mountain goats.

Satisfied by our adventure in the woods, we spent the rest of the week camping on the cliffs of Big Sur. Instead of hiking, we drove the Land Cruiser uphill, finding little turnoffs where we could camp and enjoy the view of the ocean from the tailgate. In the mornings, we made breakfast and watched the sun burn off the haze on the flat blue horizon. We spent our days driving over the mountain roads that crisscrossed the ridge. Whenever we got out to walk around, Fred would chase squirrels, and we'd gape at the gorgeous view. One day, I mountain biked while Josh walked down to the water and enjoyed the beach. At night, the sea breeze kept the bugs away, so there was no need for tents. We rolled out our sleeping mats and slept under the open sky; the bright, blinking stars were the last thing I saw each night before closing my eyes.

After a week of camping, I *really* needed a shower. My filth reminded me of a kind gesture made by a villager I had befriended in Afghanistan. In one of our last meetings, we were sitting together on a rug in his home when he jumped up and went to get something.

"He has a gift for you," my translator explained. I was surprised. We had never exchanged gifts.

The villager, a bread maker, handed me something wrapped inside a crumpled white paper napkin. He peeled back the napkin and presented me with his gift: a travel-sized bottle of shampoo. The label on the small green bottle had faded, but I think it said Pert Plus.

"For you!" the bread maker said, pointing toward my hair.

We all burst out laughing. I had been living in the dirt for weeks. We didn't have any mirrors, but I could imagine how foul I must have looked—and smelled. Here was a man who had probably never had running water encouraging me to clean up.

I thanked my friend for his gift and used it back at the compound that day. Time after time the villagers I met in Afghanistan offered us what they could. They had little but gave freely.

This time I wanted a shower, and it was a pleasure to think of my old friend back in Afghanistan.

We spent a weekend in San Francisco visiting another childhood friend then headed north toward the Redwood National and State Parks, where we hoped to do another couple of nights backpacking and camping. The drive took longer than expected, and we were losing daylight. A rusty sign by the road in Orick, California, read Last Stop For 100 Miles. As I pumped gas, Josh and I went over our options.

If we continued, we would have to start our hike in the dark, which could be dangerous. We could spend the night where we were, but there wasn't much except a gas station and a church across the street. Josh went to the tiny general store attached to the gas station to talk to someone.

"I'm either gonna come out with a place for us to sleep or a fresh box of triple-A batteries for our headlamps," he said.

After pumping gas, I leashed Fred and walked him around the parking lot. A few minutes later, the screen door of the shop slapped shut, and Josh walked toward us, followed by a gray-haired man.

"Hi there, sir," I said, shaking the man's hand.

"Name's Ed," he said. He wore overalls and cowboy boots. "Josh says you two are looking for a place to hole up for the night."

"Yes, sir. Any suggestions?" I asked.

"I work at the rodeo grounds right over there," he said, pointing across the street. "You three are welcome to pull in for the night and make camp. There are fire rings and a couple of Porta-Johns. It isn't fancy but it's the best I can do."

"That's a lot better than we could have done for ourselves," I said. "We weren't looking forward to hiking into the woods at night."

"I'd imagine not," said Ed. "If you wanna head back this way after your camping trip, we're having a rodeo in town this weekend. It'll be a good show—we have some talented riders coming in."

"Thank you, sir. We'll keep it in mind," I said, shaking Ed's hand once more. Inside the shop, we bought our provisions for the night: firewood, beef jerky, and MoonPies.

We set up camp in a large, grassy field across the street. Cattle walked lazily through the field next to ours. While we were only a few miles inland from the coast, it felt like we were a long way from the ocean. We started a fire while Fred trotted around, sniffing the grass and air curiously.

The next morning, we shook the dew from our sleeping bags while Fred watched the cattle in the distance. On our way off the grounds, Josh hopped out of the Land Cruiser and slipped a twenty-dollar bill and a thank-you note under the door of a small home near the entrance. Feeling grateful, well rested, and well fed, we headed north toward the woods.

CHAPTER 14
A BROKEN LEG

IT WAS IN the humming forest of Jedediah Smith Redwood State Park, under the peaceful, towering trees,
that Josh's leg broke.

We had hiked seven miles into the forest, weighed
down with provisions for two days. At first, the trail was
wide enough that Josh and I could walk side by side.
This was a welcome change from the hike we'd taken
the week before. Our footsteps fell into a rhythm, and
we moved so quickly that we almost forgot to appreciate the redwoods rising around us like giants.

When the trail narrowed and led us through a dry
creek bed, we stopped, stood in the shadows, looked up

at the trees. Moss covered the rough, wrinkled trunks. Even though they were in front of us, the redwoods' size was difficult to comprehend. I felt like a little kid at a grown-ups' party where all I could see were knee-caps. To walk among the towering trees took my breath away and made me feel small and insignificant.

Every time we came around a bend in the trail, we encountered bigger and more beautiful trees. My neck became tired from looking up.

It began to rain so we set up camp in a flat clear-ing. We pitched our tents, securing them in the loose gravel of the creek bed. Josh had a large tarp, and we suspended it about a foot off the ground and put our backpacks underneath to keep them dry.

The rain stopped, and Fred and I went out to explore while Josh took a nap in his tent. We kept Fred on the leash because we'd read warnings about bears and mountain lions in the area. About a mile up the creek bed, we found a fallen redwood that must have been more than two hundred feet tall. Fred and I scrambled up onto the trunk. We stood and got our bearings, then ran across like kids on a playground. With his low center of gravity, Fred had no trouble balancing. He scurried back and forth over the trunk, often looking back at me, mouth open, ears perked, eyes wide.

When we climbed down, we looked into the woods.

The afternoon sun broke through the rain clouds and warmed us while we rested. I paused to appreciate the moment: I was standing beside a centuries-old redwood tree in California with my stray dog from Afghanistan. It seemed like we'd been destined to end up here.

When Fred and I returned to camp, we found Josh sitting on a log slamming his prosthetic leg against the log.

"Hey, man. What happened?" I asked.

"Some dirt found its way in and jammed up my knee," Josh said. "Stupid thing is supposed to be used in the field. I put the dust cover on and everything."

Josh said that he had knelt down in the creek bed to pick up the tarp, and gravel got into the joint of his prosthetic knee. When he stood up, the leg jammed and he lost his footing, falling onto his elbow and pushing more gravel into the knee's exposed mechanics. He was trying to clear the tiny pebbles and dirt from the joint with a small brush meant for cleaning the inside of a rifle. A trail of blood ran down his forearm from where he'd fallen on his elbow.

I had never seen Josh like this. He always stayed calm, but now his body tensed with frustration. He may not have realized he was bleeding. The leg hummed like an electric razor, and Josh's fingers were raw from digging at the robotic hinge of the knee. I fastened Fred's leash to a nearby tree and took a seat across from him.

"Why's it humming like that?" I asked.

"I have no idea," Josh said. "I've never heard it do that before."

He took a deep breath. "The good news is that I got out all of the rocks and got it to stand up straight again. The bad news is that the knee is completely shot. Now it's essentially a really expensive peg leg."

"Okay," I said, pausing to think. Josh had become quite good at hiking on the uneven, treacherous trails we'd been on. He had made it through the brush in the Los Padres National Forest without problems, but the knee had broken from his simply kneeling on the ground.

We didn't have many options. Josh had a backup leg in the Land Cruiser, but we had to get to it and then charge it.

"What if we hike out tomorrow morning and take our time?" I said. It was already getting late in the day. "That way you don't strain your good leg."

Josh agreed, and we settled into camp for the night. We heated our dinners and sat around the campsite until dusk. As we ate and talked, Josh decided that after our trip he would call one of the prosthetic manufacturer's representatives with suggestions to change the design.

Before it got dark, Fred and I walked away from camp and hung our food from a distant tree to keep it out of reach from curious wildlife. When we returned, Josh had already gone to bed.

That night, a storm rolled in. Light drops of rain pitter-pattered against the tent. Fred and I lay safe and dry under a blanket as the rain sang us to sleep.

When the morning sun filtered through the giant trees, the sunlight woke us. Outside, Josh fiddled with his leg while Fred and I went to retrieve the food I'd strung up the night before. I saw huge paw prints in the dirt beneath the bag. They could have only been made by a bear. I untied the knot from around the trunk of the tree and let the bag fall to the ground. It had been untouched but not unnoticed.

When we got back to camp, Josh was too focused on adjusting to his leg to care much about the bear tracks. He knew the seven-mile hike back to the truck was going to hurt.

"Just go, man," Josh said. He didn't want to hold me up.

"Listen, there's no rush," I said. "I'll go in front. If you start to go down, try to fall forward onto my pack so you can catch yourself."

We stepped onto the trail. Almost immediately, it seemed more challenging than it had on the way in.

The rain had turned the soil to mud and made the rocks slippery. The path seemed treacherous now that Josh was essentially hiking with one leg. His prosthetic knee could give out if he put too much weight on it. I tried to keep an even pace, pausing every so often to check on Josh.

When we reached the creek crossing, we knew there was only a mile left to go. Josh picked up the pace, even passing Fred and me in a combination of determination and frustration. He hadn't fallen yet, and I knew he couldn't wait to get to the Land Cruiser and take off his broken leg.

At the end of the trail, Fred and I caught up to him, and together, the three of us walked out of the redwoods, the same way we'd come in. We got to the Land Cruiser, and I dropped the tailgate as fast as I could so Josh could get off his feet. He took a seat and removed his leg while I poured Fred a big bowl of cool water from the cooler. We'd made it.

We drove north into Oregon, only to find that the campsite where we planned to stay was full. We asked for directions to a place where we could get something to eat and charge Josh's leg. At about three o'clock in the afternoon we ended up at the Blue Moon Saloon and Café, where Josh sat down near an outlet and started to charge his backup leg.

We ate sandwiches and potato chips while waiting for the three little LED lights on Josh's leg to go from blinking to solid green, the sign it was fully charged. Our next destination was Crater Lake, a few hours west, but we realized we needed to find a place to stay for the night. We were running low on cash, so we called around looking for another campground. We didn't have any luck.

At about five o'clock, a woman in jeans, boots, and a flannel shirt sat down near us, clearly waiting for someone. We asked her if she knew a nearby campground.

"You two just passing through?" she asked, explaining that there was no room at the campsite outside of town.

I told her we were two veterans taking the summer to drive across the country, introducing my Afghan dog to America. I pointed to the Land Cruiser, parked just outside the window, where Fred was resting in the back seat, enjoying the cool ocean breeze. Fred looked happy as ever in his prime people-watching spot.

The woman glanced from Fred to me. "I'm Ashley," she said, extending her hand to shake ours. A bearded guy in a hoodie and baseball cap walked in and came over to us.

We introduced ourselves. His name was Chris.

"When Ashley texted and told me she was talking to two veterans at the bar, I assumed it was two old guys."

We laughed.

"What brings you guys into our little town?" Chris asked. "Is this a stop on the run-down-town tour?"

"We heard you guys had the best electricity in Oregon," Josh joked, looking over his shoulder at his prosthetic leg leaned up against the wall. By now, two of the lights were solid green.

"Whoa!" said Chris in what appeared to be genuine shock. "That looks like something out of *The Terminator*!"

Ashley started to apologize, but we were laughing too hard to care. The four of us continued to joke around and talk. We learned that Ashley handled billing and orders for a local logging company and Chris worked half the year in fishing and the other half in logging. Josh and I told them about our road trip so far.

"Well, your experience in the redwoods explains why you both smell like bear farts," Chris said.

"What he means to say is that if you two want to, you're more than welcome to stay the night at my place," Ashley said. "You can do laundry in the morning and get cleaned up. We don't have much but we'd love to have you."

Josh and I were stunned. The thought of doing

laundry and sleeping indoors sounded fantastic. We'd run out of friends to stay with until we got to Seattle, where we planned to stay with one of Josh's army buddies.

I tried to protest, but Ashley insisted. "My two boys are with their father this weekend so we have room," she said. "You can sleep in our camper. That's where they like to play, so you'll just have to excuse the mess. This is really all for Fred, anyway. I can't wait to meet him and spoil him."

We slept soundly in the camper. The space felt luxurious, especially compared to our tents. I crawled up onto a loft bed, Josh took the bed in the back, and Fred lay on a couch seat. In the morning, I awoke to the squeal of the door as it opened. Ashley pressed her fingers to her lips as she crept in. "Just grabbing your laundry," she whispered. "Breakfast will be ready in an hour, sleepyheads."

I didn't know how we'd repay her for her hospitality. The smell of bacon wafted into the camper. Her home was a single-story ranch on a big stretch of land. A long gravel driveway led to the house, and dirt bike trails created by Ashley's boys stretched from the house back to the woods.

When we entered the kitchen, we found fresh mugs of coffee waiting for us. Ashley buzzed around, flipping bacon and pulling hot toast from a toaster. "Have a seat!" she said.

Ashley mixed together some rice, eggs, and bacon for Fred. She placed it in front of him, then stood and slid our plates in front of us: bacon, eggs, toast, and home fries, along with her special homemade hot sauce. Until that moment, I thought I had fine breakfast-making skills, but I had a lot to learn if I wanted to make anything as good as what Ashley put in front of us. It was delicious.

Later, Ashley and Chris took us to the best seafood place in town. Josh and I planned to head to a beach to camp. We were overwhelmed by Chris and Ashley's kindness and didn't want to overstay our welcome.

Back at the house, Josh and I packed up the Land Cruiser while Fred circled our feet. Ashley walked over with two plastic shopping bags and set them down on the tailgate.

"Now, you two aren't gonna leave here without this, and I won't take no for an answer," she said.

From one of the bags, she reached in and lifted out a mason jar to show us.

"We caught this tuna a few months ago. I cooked it and canned it on the spot. It's better than anything you two are gonna eat on the road and certainly better than anything you'll find in a store," she said. "I added a box of saltines and a bottle of my homemade hot sauce in there for you, too."

She tied the first bag shut. From the second bag, she pulled out something I'd never seen before.

"These are firebugs," she said. "I made a bunch for my boys' Scout troop but they didn't use 'em all. Place one in the middle of some dry kindling and it'll get your fire going."

I was impressed. The firebugs were genius. To make them, Ashley had taken the bottom of a cardboard egg carton and cut it into individual pieces. She had filled each compartment with wood shavings from the saw-mill where she worked and sealed the top by dripping candle wax. Each firebug was a pocket-sized fire starter.

"These will burn forever!" I said.

"We thought we were seasoned campers by now, but you just put us in our place," Josh said. "I bet you could light a fire in the rain with one of these."

Ashley laughed then hugged us. We were grateful for the gifts, but I knew the most important thing we'd take away from our time with Ashley was the memory of her kindness. Without asking anything in return— or knowing much about us—she'd opened the doors to her home, taken us in, and taken care of us.

Next stop: camping at Crater Lake. Fred and I woke up in our tent, the ground vibrating and the canvas of the tent shaking like Jell-O. Fred looked confused, his eyebrows lifted and head tilted. After a few seconds, I realized it was an earthquake. I'd experienced a few while I was training in California, but they were quicker and more violent. This one rumbled for almost a minute, as if gently lulling us out of our sleep.

Once it stilled, we climbed out of our tent and discovered that it had snowed overnight. The dusting of white made the landscape dreamlike and beautiful.

Josh, Fred, and I spent the day hiking around the lake. The more we climbed, the hotter it got, making the mysterious morning snowfall seem like a hallucination. After hiking for twelve miles, we took one final journey, a mile-long path down to the water's edge. All day, Josh had done well on his backup leg. We moved at a good clip, and I almost forgot about the long, intense struggle of the redwoods. If Josh was in any pain, he didn't say anything.

We reached a cliff about twenty-five feet above the water. The blue water was deep enough to jump, but Josh would need to make sure he vaulted far enough out to avoid getting snagged by the rocks on the way down. It was not the same as dropping off the log like we'd done in Los Padres.

"Hold my leg," Josh said.

Josh sat down and popped off his prosthetic. A crowd of people stood nearby to watch people jump from that spot. When Josh removed his leg, the crowd stared. Josh balanced on the edge. I knelt on all fours beside him so he could use my back for balance, then push himself forward. I felt Josh's cold, dry hand on my shoulder. I was about to ask if he wanted me to count down when, without warning, Josh launched himself up and out.

He soared through the air, leg first, arms out, in total free fall. When he splashed into the water, he slipped deep beneath its smooth, reflective surface. A moment later, he reappeared, blowing out a mouthful of water and smiling widely. Everybody around us cheered. I hadn't realized until then how closely the crowd was watching.

Fred climbed down the rocks to meet Josh at the bottom, making sure he was okay. I followed, Josh's prosthetic in hand, smiling.

CHAPTER 15
CHANGE OF PLANS

OUR NEXT STOP wasn't part of the plan: we were headed to a Veterans Affairs hospital in Seattle. Josh's prosthetic leg was fine, but his good leg was giving him problems. He thought he might have a blood clot, which could be life-threatening.

We had stopped in Portland, Oregon, and for the last few days, Josh had been leaning into his prosthetic more than usual, limping a little. Josh finally told me he was in pain, but it was clear that he had been uncomfortable for a while. I thought about all the demanding hiking we'd done in Big Sur, the redwoods, and Crater Lake, wondering if we'd pushed too hard.

We planned to stay in Seattle with Matt, another of Josh's army friends. When we pulled up to his apartment, Matt met us outside. He looked like he could have been Josh's brother: they were both tall and thin, with big smiles and similar mannerisms. Matt had been one of the medics in Josh's unit. Now he was in the Army Reserve and had a civilian job as an X-ray technician at a local hospital.

We joked around for a bit and then I told Matt what was going on. "We should get Josh to the hospital," I said. "His leg is getting worse."

We dropped our gear with Matt, and I drove Josh to the VA hospital. Neither of us spoke. I knew Josh feared that someday he'd have to have his good leg amputated. It had been badly damaged. He had shown me the scars where shrapnel had sliced through muscle and surgeons had made repairs.

I went out of my way to treat Josh the same way I would have treated any of my other buddies. I didn't want him to feel that I doubted him or babied him because of his prosthetic. If we were on a trail and he needed to rest, I'd sit with him and wait. I didn't ask, "Are you okay?" with pity or worry. I knew he wanted to push himself, and I wanted to help him do that.

Now that something was wrong, it was hard to find the right words. Josh had challenged himself throughout his recovery, and especially on our trip. He'd been a good friend, listening to me tell Fred's story over and over again, waiting for me when I wanted to mountain bike, and putting up with me for two months on the road.

When we got to the VA, I gave Josh a quick hug.

"Hey, man, at least you know your way around a VA hospital," I said. "You should be able to get seen pretty quick." Josh knew I was being sarcastic. No appointment at the VA could ever be described as "quick."

"Yeah, bro, I'll be in and out," Josh said, not looking at me. "Go have fun with Matt. He's a great guy." He rubbed Fred's head and let the dog lick his face before hopping out of the truck.

Fred and I watched Josh limp down the breezeway and through the lobby doors. I drove back to Matt's house to wait for an update from Josh. On the drive, Fred didn't climb into Josh's seat like he usually would have. Instead, he stayed in the back with his head down, as if he knew something wasn't right. In the past two months, our pack had never separated. I wanted to feel optimistic, but I had a sinking feeling that this was where Josh's trip ended.

"You know, if it is a blood clot, it's a good thing you stopped in Portland," Matt said.

"What do you mean it's good we stopped in

Portland?" I asked. We were sitting at the dog park watching Fred and Matt's white Labrador, Lucy, chase each other.

"Clots usually get worse when someone sits still for an extended period of time," he said. "If you had driven all the way up to Seattle, one of the clots could have traveled up to Josh's brain or his heart. That could have killed him." Matt spoke in the matter-of-fact tone of medical professionals.

I hadn't understood how bad things could have been. We'd come so far on our trip, and our difficulties had been relatively minor. Maybe our luck was running out.

I got Fred settled at Matt's house and went back to the hospital. I didn't want Josh to feel alone.

Under the fluorescent lights in the hospital lobby, I bought a cup of coffee from a vending machine and took a seat in a stiff plastic chair. A few elderly veterans wearing Vietnam vet baseball caps sat in wheelchairs or with walkers. The group appeared to be waiting for a bus back to their assisted living facility. I didn't speak to any of them, but I was reminded of the shameful ways the veterans of that era were treated when they came home. Many of them had been drafted into the conflict and saw combat that left them physically and mentally scarred. The society they'd returned to was a far cry from our current thank-you-for-your-service spirit. I tried to remember that anytime I found myself complaining about the VA.

I got a text from Josh: "Blood clots. They wrote me a prescription. I'll be out in ten."

I was relieved that Josh didn't need to stay in the hospital, but I knew we weren't out of the woods. About twenty minutes later, he came out carrying a shopping bag of meds. He had been prescribed pain meds and a blood thinner that he needed to inject into his leg twice a day.

He still limped but he was smiling.

"Hey, man, you didn't have to wait for me," he said.

"Well, I really wanted to get a look at the lobby of the Seattle VA," I said. "It was right up there on my must-see list with the Grand Canyon and the redwoods."

Josh climbed into the Land Cruiser. "I never thought I'd be so happy to see the inside of this beauty," Josh said. "The doctor told me to take it easy but she didn't say anything about not traveling."

I had assumed he'd catch the next flight home. "If you wanna keep going, it's your call," I said. "I just don't want you to drop dead on me. That would really kill the trip."

"I always thought my time would come in the passenger seat of a Land Cruiser—I just didn't think it'd be this soon," he said.

❧ ❧ ❧

Josh and I had our first big fight a few days later in Minneapolis. One of Josh's high school friends took us to a Twins game. All night, I noticed Josh favoring one leg and limping. I was concerned, especially because we were low on money and ready to drive back to Washington, DC.

"Hey, man. You feeling okay?" I asked. "How's your leg?" I tried to sound casual.

"Yeah—I'm fine," Josh said. "Why?"

"You just looked a little uncomfortable while we were walking around tonight," I said. "I realized I hadn't really asked you about your leg in a while."

Things had been tense between us since Seattle. After saying goodbye to Matt, we drove ten long hours to Bozeman, Montana. We camped overnight, and I went for a long mountain bike ride, then it was onward to North Dakota and Minneapolis. I felt a strain between us that hadn't been there before.

I thought Josh was putting his health at risk. We both knew he'd done more on this trip than we thought possible. Why didn't he know when to call it quits? I wanted Josh to appreciate the difference between challenging himself and being reckless. He was ignoring his pain. To me, his problem was obvious. What was much harder for me to see was that I was ignoring my own pain, too.

"Look. Why don't you just say it? You think I should fly home," Josh said. "I can tell you've been thinking it."

"Shouldn't you listen to the doctors in Seattle?" I asked. "Didn't they say riding in the car could be bad for the clots? That's pretty much all we're gonna do between here and DC."

"If you want me off the trip, just say it," he said.

After months on the road together, we were on each other's nerves.

"I want you to make that decision," I said. "I want you to take a look at your situation and deal with it instead of sweeping it under the rug and making it someone else's problem."

I didn't hold back. "This summer you've seen what you're capable of—how far you can push yourself mentally and physically. Now you need to accept your limitations."

The next morning, I drove Josh to the airport. We got out at the departure terminal and stood next to the Land Cruiser. Cars whizzed past and people hurried through revolving doors. I handed Josh his duffel bag and gave him a hug.

"Thanks, man," Josh said. "I had a great time."

He kissed Fred on the head.

"I couldn't have done it without you," I said. "I'm

really glad you came." It was true.

In the front seat, Fred didn't whimper or complain. He seemed to understand that Josh needed to go. I shifted the Land Cruiser into gear and headed toward home.

CHAPTER 16
HOME

ON A HOT AFTERNOON in mid-August not long after I got
home from the road trip, Josh helped me move into a
house near Georgetown University. I didn't have much
to move: just a desk, mattress, small fridge, footlocker,
and an old thrift-store chair Fred loved to sleep in. I
also still had a few of Josh's things, including the leg
that broke in the redwoods.

Josh showed up with a clean shave and fresh haircut.
He was interviewing for jobs.

After lugging furniture up to my room, we sat out on
the back porch. The deck overlooked a small fenced-in
backyard with patches of grass and bricks. We watched

parents moving their kids into college housing units around us.

We talked about the year ahead, how Josh was looking for a job and I was looking forward to starting classes and playing ice hockey. We talked about the trip and how parts felt almost like being in the military.

"I feel like a jerk for the things I said in Minneapolis," I said. I wanted to clear the air. "I was out of line trying to tell you how to deal with your issues."

During our argument, I had told Josh not to let his injury become the most interesting thing about him. I had been too harsh.

"You weren't wrong about it," Josh said. "I definitely saw what I can do this summer. I know I need to value my time here and not just coast through it."

"We both need to make sure we never forget that," I said.

Josh helped me recognize things in myself. We didn't want to be considered victims because of what we'd been through in Afghanistan. We'd both had near-death experiences and seen our friends die, and we knew we were lucky to be alive. That's why we pushed ourselves so hard. The challenge kept us moving forward.

We were both so used to saying we were "fine" that it had become difficult to admit when we weren't. We didn't want our friends and families to treat us differently, but the truth was that some things about us were different. Josh and I were both trying to figure out how to live fulfilling lives after the military.

"I think it'll be a long time before we know just how important this summer was," Josh said.

I knew he was right.

In the spring of 2016, I graduated from Georgetown University with a Bachelor of Arts in Liberal Studies and a concentration in International Affairs. I didn't know what I was supposed to do next. I heard my dad's words in my head: "You've got a degree now. You need to focus on getting back to work in a stable job with a future." He wasn't wrong, but I wasn't sure what I wanted to do.

I didn't want to return to a conventional job. I was terrified that I would find myself sixty years old and not feeling proud of what I'd done with my life.

Before the road trip, I'd met a girl named Nora. She was a musician—creative, outgoing, and incredibly pretty, with a smile that lit up the room. We'd kept in touch, sharing updates about our lives and checking in with each other. Before my final semester at Georgetown, we started dating, and after graduation we moved in together. The four of us became a family:

Nora, Nora's dog Ruby (an energetic little terrier mix), Fred, and me.

Nora worked an office job that paid the bills while I worked at a men's clothing store and tried to figure out what to do with my life. I applied for a job with a high-profile government contractor. I went through round after round of interviews. Finally, they made me an offer. Before I could commit, I had to reinstate my security clearance, which had lapsed while I was in school.

As summer turned into fall, I began planning the fourth annual memorial fund-raiser event in Justin's honor. I had started it in 2013 after a friend who had heard me talk about Justin encouraged me to hold an event on the anniversary of his death. I called Justin's wife, Ann, who lived in Pittsburgh, and she recommended that the donations be given to TAPS—the Tragedy Assistance Program for Survivors—a nonprofit that provides grief counseling to families of military members and emergency responders who have died.

The first year I made T-shirts that said SCHMALLS on the front—Justin's nickname—and had a Bruce Lee quote on the back: "Real living is living for others." A friend of mine who owned a bar hosted the event and all the proceeds of the night went to TAPS. The event became bigger and bigger each year.

The year I graduated, Justin's parents agreed to come for the first time. I had joined a cover band as the drummer, and we planned to play for the night. I was anxious but determined to make it a memorable event—the best one yet.

Then, I got a call from the company that had offered me the intelligence job. To get the job, I needed to pass a polygraph test, which was scheduled for the morning after Justin's fund-raiser. I called them immediately and asked to reschedule, even explaining I was hosting an event for a friend who had been killed in action.

"Sorry, but we don't reschedule polygraphs," the representative said. "That's your date."

We had scheduled the fund-raiser for the Wednesday night after Thanksgiving. It was cold and rainy, and ticket presales hadn't been great. I was nervous. I showed up that afternoon to set up. We made signs, decorated, and arranged the T-shirt table. At seven PM, when the doors opened, Justin's parents were the first to arrive. The venue manager, who also happened to be a marine veteran, met them at the door and showed them inside. When he told me they were there, my heart pounded.

Keep it together, man, I thought. I introduced myself and held out my hand to Justin's dad, John. He looked at my hand and said, "No, I'm a hugger." He pulled me in for a bear hug.

Justin's mom, Deborah, had a quiet confidence that reminded me of Justin.

My dad joined us and the conversation turned to Pittsburgh. I told them how Justin's accent had been the first thing I'd picked up on. As we talked, I watched the crowd grow. Josh was there, as well as friends from my former job, including my former commanding officer and the sniper I used to eat lunch with. Friends from the military showed up, in addition to a number of my high school buddies. Ten minutes before the show started, the entire Georgetown club hockey team appeared with a bunch of their friends in tow. People from nearly every corner of my life had come together and were gathered all in one place.

After we played the first set, my friend who owned the bar made some remarks. "This is one of my favorite nights of the year," he said. "We're all here to think about someone who left us too soon." He introduced Justin's dad, John.

"Justin would have been totally overwhelmed with all of this attention," John said. "But it means a lot to me and my family to see all of you here and to know my son's memory isn't gone. Thank you."

Through tears, I got up and thanked everyone in the room for being there. After we finished playing, I spent the rest of the night by John's side, listening to funny stories about Justin as a kid and about his wedding day.

I went to bed that night exhausted, but feeling that I had done something important.

Before leaving for the fund-raiser that afternoon, I had arranged my suit on the bed to prepare for the polygraph the next morning. Moving forward with the new job made a lot of sense: it would offer a good income, a clear career path, and a sensible retirement account. It was the practical choice.

It was also the kind of choice I had avoided my entire life. If I had lived my life the practical way, I wouldn't have joined the marines, gone to Afghanistan, or met Justin. I wouldn't have moved to the city, enrolled at Georgetown, or gone on the road trip. And I wouldn't have Fred.

The morning after Justin's fund-raiser, I skipped the polygraph test. Instead, I wrote an email about Fred and sent it to a website called The Dodo, knowing they published unusual and uplifting stories about animals. The next day, the editor published an article about Fred and me, along with a video of our story. An editor at a publishing house saw that post and asked me to write a book—the book you are reading.

I had done a lot of academic writing in school, but I wanted to share something more personal. I thought it would help me make sense of what I'd been through. At first I didn't know how to write about war or the marines or my time in Afghanistan, and then I realized the right place to start was with Fred.

Fred and I have been through a lot together, both in Afghanistan and at home. He has taught me a lot about life and about myself.

Fred has taught me that a loving, adventurous, and rewarding life is possible if I choose to be optimistic.

He has reminded me to love unconditionally and joyfully.

He has given me the strength to face my challenges, even when I haven't wanted to.

He has helped me learn not to take a moment of my life for granted. He has shown me the power of stubborn positivity and what is possible when I understand that it is not what happens to me, but how I react, that matters.

Fred came into my life when I needed him most. I rescued Fred once, but he has rescued me again and again.

IN MEMORIAM

IN HONOR OF
SEAN OSTERMAN AND JUSTIN SCHMALSTIEG,
THEIR PARENTS SHARE THEIR LOVE AND MEMORIES.

Gunnery Sergeant Justin E. Schmalstieg
May 16, 1982–December 15, 2010

SINCE HE WAS a young boy, we knew Justin was destined to be someone special. Justin was noticeably independent at an early age. He was full of life and had a great love for his family, which was evident when his brother John Jr. was born. You could see that instant bond between the two of them. Justin also had a great love and respect for his friends, who in turn showed the same love and respect; he was someone they could look up to.

As Justin grew, he pursued and began dating his one true love, his soul mate, Ann. When Justin graduated high school, he went on to complete one semester at

Penn State, then he decided to join the Marine Corps because he said he liked "the way the uniform looked." Several years after joining the Marine Corps, he eventually captured Ann's heart forever, and they were married on November 7, 2009.

Justin served three tours of duty in Iraq and one in Afghanistan. Throughout his career with the Marine Corps, Justin was known as a comic, but he also had the respect of his superiors and subordinates, and he gave back the same respect until God decided he needed another angel on December 15, 2010.

We are very thankful to everyone, especially Craig, for keeping Justin's memory alive. Not a day goes by without thoughts of Justin. He is forever in our hearts.

Justin's parents,
John M. Gilkey Sr.
Deborah L. Gilkey

Corporal Sean A. Osterman
January 11, 1989–December 16, 2010

WITH SEAN, THINGS ALWAYS had a flair about them. He was born three weeks late, and at just a day old, he was able to hold his head up. As he grew, he wanted to run, and that's what he did: T-ball, soccer, swimming, lacrosse, karate, and anything that would wear him out. Sean had an active mind, too. He tested at a college reading level in sixth grade and scored 100 percent on his state testing in eighth-grade math.

At age fifteen, Sean was already six feet tall and wanted to join the military. As a junior, he joined the marines in the delayed entry program. He graduated from high school in 2007 and left for boot camp that summer. Even after suffering a stress fracture in his leg and limping through graduation, he never gave up.

After completing his first tour in Afghanistan, Sean extended his enlistment in order to go on his final deployment. He offered to take the place of a fellow marine who had just had a baby girl with his wife.

When we reached Sean in Germany, we were informed that he was gone but still on life support until our arrival. When we were asked about his viable organs, it was the only time I could hear that baritone voice of his in my mind: "Hell yes, Mom." Sean's organs saved four people on December 18, 2010. His heart is still beating in Germany, a gift that has sustained us in some dark times.

Sean's mother,
Kelly Rae Hugo

ACKNOWLEDGMENTS

Kelly Shetron, coauthor: I am endlessly proud of the work we have done. Thank you for being a consistent and professional coauthor in this effort to share Fred's story. Thank you for helping me make sense of my journey and for shaping it in a way that makes me appear a much better writer than I am. Fred and I are proud to call you our friend.

Chad Luibl, my literary agent and best friend: Your professionalism and tenacity are the only reason our story has received the attention it deserves. Thank you for being my voice and the strongest advocate for Fred and me since day one. In some ways we have come a long way from the playground at Fairview Elementary and our street hockey games in the cul-de-sacs of Burke, Virginia. In more important ways, however, we are still the same. Thank you.

Rachel Kahan, William Morrow: Thank you for understanding from the very beginning how special Fred's story is, and for matching my enthusiasm. Thank you for your expert editorial eye, and for giving me the freedom to work as well as the guidance I needed to work well. And Fred wishes to thank you for treating him like the VIP he thinks he is (and also for the gourmet dog treats you always offer him).

Rosemary Brosnan and Courtney Stevenson, Harper-Collins Children's: Thank you for helping me share Fred's story with what is probably his most important audience, and for all the energy, enthusiasm, and joy you exude in our every interaction.

Winifred Conkling: Thank you for your hard work and commitment in shaping our story so that it is accessible for a young audience. You have created the type of book I would've skipped recess to read.

Eve Claxton, writing guru: Thank you for your editorial guidance and your ever-positive energy. Thank you for taking the time to understand my story, and for helping me share it in its best form.

And many thanks to Kate Schafer, Gena Lanzi,

Liate Stehlik, Lynn Grady, Kaitlin Harri, Emma Parry, Michael Steger, and the rest of "Team Fred" at William Morrow, HarperCollins Children's, and Janklow & Nesbit Associates. You all are a part of this, and I am grateful for your hard work.

Honora Parkington, Director of Fred Operations/ Girl of My Dreams: You believed in my writing long before you had any reason to. You saw something in me that I thought I had lost, and you helped me find it again. I can't imagine my life without you and I'm so glad that I don't have to. I love you.

Sarah: Thank you for always telling me I was smart, even when I felt stupid. Thank you for never doubting me, even when I doubted myself. Thank you for reminding me that I'll always be your little brother, even though I look so much older than you. And most of all, thank you for helping me sneak a dog out of Afghanistan, even when I thought I couldn't.

Dad: Thank you for being my example of what it means to be a man. Because of you I understand the importance of selflessly serving my community, my country, and the world. You taught me the value of hard work, and you inspired me to become the man I am today.

Mom: Thank you for trusting me, even when it terrified you. Thank you for guiding me when it seemed like I wasn't listening. Thank you for making me laugh, sometimes when there was little reason to. Thank you for always believing in me in those times when I didn't believe in myself.

Nonnie: Thank you for being the toughest and most loving lady I've ever met, for teaching me how to be honest and brave. Thank you for your endless love and support.

Jason B.: Thank you for your dedication to my sister and the wonderful family you two have created. Your work ethic and adaptability are of a superhuman caliber.

Maurice: Thank you for your endless support and for being an example to me of class, grace, and Belgian hospitality. Thank you for loving my family and taking care of my mom.

Bren: Thank you for helping to take care of Fred, and for loving my family and always treating me like your son. Thank you for loving my dad and keeping him young.

Josh: Thank you for coming on the road trip with Fred and me. It would not have been the same without you. Thank you for being an example of friendship and brotherhood. Thank you for all your help with this book and for always believing in our story.

Ysa: My friend and brother, you're the kind of

person that I brag about knowing. Thank you for always being a phone call away, no matter how far a distance you might actually be. Thank you for being equal parts goofball and badass. You're an amazing husband, father, and friend.

Bobby: Thank you for getting shot in the arm so you could come and hang out with us in Sangin, and thank you for putting your art career on hold to be a marine for a while. I'm proud to have served with you and I'm proud to be your friend.

Dave: "Thank you for kicking that guy in the chest, and for always letting me sleep in your sleeping bag, and for not getting mad when I hid that donkey leg on your pillow. Love, Fred."

Jason: "Thank you for making me my first collar. Even though I didn't like it, I know you worked hard on it. Thank you for petting me and defending me from those mean guys that day. Love, Fred."

Mark (Top): Thank you for being one of Fred's first friends, and for helping me stuff him into that duffel bag and bring him home. Thank you for showing us what it is to be a leader worth following.

Joe: Thanks for your contributions to the book and for being a friend to Fred and me. I am proud to have served with you.

Adam: Thank you for not treating me like an attachment. Thank you for your friendship and for your leadership. I am proud to have served with you.

The marines of First and Second Recon: Thank you for letting me contribute to your mission and for your daily demonstrations of bravery and kindness. I am proud to have served with every one of you.

Tony: Thank you for taking the time to listen to me, even when you couldn't understand me. Thank you for carrying Stroh's even when nobody wanted to drink it. Thank you for helping me honor my friends. I am proud to call The Pug home and I am proud to call you my friend.

Chaz: Thank you giving me the courage to share the memory and story of Justin. Thank you for listening to me and reminding me what good music is. I can't wait to see how big we can make Schmalls Fest. I'm proud to call you my friend.

Georgetown hockey program: Thank you for giving this old bruiser another shot at glory, and for reminding me how special this game we play is. It is an honor to have won and lost beside each of you. Thank you for your continued support and friendship.

My DIA friends: Thank you for getting water with me every twenty minutes and for listening to my stories about Fred, no matter how many times you'd heard them. Your presence made every day a bit brighter, and I loved working with you.

Bill: Thank you for being my first friend in the

marines and for showing me that I could be a marine while still being myself. Thank you for helping me with my school papers and not calling me out for all the times I swore I'd never go to college.

PJ: Thank you for always believing in Fred's story, for inspiring me to share it, and for helping me see the value in being a writer instead of an intel guy. Thank you for helping me move apartments more times than I can remember.

My friends: Thank you for always treating me the same no matter how different I might feel on the inside. Thank you for standing by me and not being afraid to tell me when I'm wrong. Thank you for being awesome to one another and for only growing up the appropriate amount.

Dog friends: To anyone who has casually asked me, "What kind of dog is that?" in a dog park, campsite, street corner, or hotel lobby, thank you for listening and recognizing that Fred is more than a dog to me. Most of all, thank you for not calling him a corgi.

Fred's social media supporters all over the world: We would not be here without you. Many of you have believed in our story from the very beginning. You have provided the support and validation we needed to keep going, and the positive stories you've shared have been a true inspiration. Thank you.